LETTERS TO A

YOUNG GAY

CHRISTIAN

Aaron Walsh

To Ann Marie,

Always remember that
you are loved!

Love,
Aaron

For my family and for young people everywhere

TABLE OF CONTENTS

LETTER OF INTRODUCTION

"Come to me, all you who labor and are burdened, and I will give you rest. Take my yoke upon you and learn from me, for I am meek and humble of heart; and you will find rest for yourselves. For my yoke is easy, and my burden light."

- Matthew 11: 28-30, The New American Bible

Dear Brother, Dear Sister, Dear Friend,

Thank you for having the courage to give this book a try. When I first realized that I might be gay, I was too afraid to talk to anyone about it. I was even too embarrassed and ashamed to check out books about homosexuality from the local library. I was terrified that someone might see what I was reading and make all kinds of assumptions. Over time, I struggled to reconcile different parts of myself. My religion, which I loved, had taught me to internalize negative beliefs about same-sex relationships. It felt like different parts of myself were at war with each other. I was a Christian and a gay man, an intellectual and an artist, a servant and a rebel. It took me a long time to learn that these elements of my identity were not opposing extremes, but rather gifts given to me by God. They were all important parts of who I was made to be, and they fit together as God intended from the beginning.

I learned a lot about life over the years through prayer and loving relationships with family, friends, colleagues, and mentors. And I learned a lot from reading books about religion and sexual orientation. The works I found usually approached these subjects from either an intellectual point of view or as accounts of personal experiences. For example, I found great books that explored Biblical passages about homosexuality through a historical lens, and there were compelling stories written by gay Christians about their own lives.

But for a long time, I felt lost. What I really needed was a book that spoke directly to me in my pain, confusion, loneliness, hopes, and dreams. I had a difficult time finding a community where I felt like I truly belonged. As an avid reader, I always found peace in the realms opened through literature and spiritual texts. Thus as a young gay Christian, I yearned to read something that spoke God's truth of love and mercy directly to me. I wanted evidence that the Word made flesh loved me despite my gayness, or even because of it. I wanted to believe that God could still live through my life, that I could still be a blessing to others and an advocate for justice in the world.

After years of deep thought and prayer, I decided to write the book I so desperately needed to read. You have before you a collection of pastoral letters written to a young gay Christian. Each chapter is a letter intended for a certain moment in life, a certain point in time. You can read this book cover to cover or flip through it to the message you need today. Even if all my words are worthless, I encourage you to spend time meditating on the Scripture passages that are woven throughout this book. Our Bible holds words of truth inspired by the Holy Spirit. We need to educate ourselves, pray, and talk with loving people to understand what the Scriptures mean, but we can ultimately trust that these sacred books carry messages of hope and love for all people of all times. I hope this book of letters brings you comfort and peace as you grow into the person God wants you to be.

As you will soon find out, I open each letter to my brother, sister, and friend. In doing so, I hope to make a personal connection with you, my fellow person of faith, and also honor the diverse gender identities of my readers. God is Ultimate Being and, as such, is beyond human conceptions of gender. Yet for me, there is something very personal and endearing about pronouns in the English language. I believe that God wants above all to be in loving, intimate relationship with each of us. For these reasons, I alternate between using He/Him and She/Her pronouns while referring to God the Creator. To keep things in balance, I consistently refer to Jesus Christ with he/him pronouns and to the Holy Spirit using she/her pronouns. Of course, there are infinite options for gender pronouns and one can happily use only personal names without pronouns. I encourage everyone to prayerfully consider the pronouns, names, and titles they choose to use or not use for God.

When I address this book to someone "young," I mean anyone who is on the journey to find out who they are and how they want to live. At the end of the day, we are all young in the light of eternity, and so this book can be for anyone of any age. By gay, I mean anyone whose sexual orientation or gender identity does not fit the culturally-expected heterosexual and cisgender mold. (By cisgender, I mean a person who identifies with the gender they were assumed to be at birth.) Whoever you tend to be romantically and sexually drawn to, this book is for you. Whether you identify with the gender that was assigned to you at birth or a different gender, or whether you feel gender is not relevant to you or that you are a unique or fluid combination of multiple genders, this book is for you. As a gay cisgender man, the insights related in this book weigh heavily on matters related to sexual orientation over gender identity simply because of my personal experiences. If in ignorance I have written something insensitive, inaccurate, or hurtful, I apologize. Furthermore, I hope this book contains some elements of God's truth, which is universal and for all peoples. While this book has a focused mission to provide support and encouragement for young gay Christians, I hope that everyone, including straight cisgender people of all religions, can find in its pages wisdom, truth, and the warmth of a fellow human being trying to write a little love into the world. At the end of the day, I want all of us to live in peaceful community with the Holy Spirit of God dwelling in our hearts.

Ultimately, this book is a fruit of my relationship with Jesus Christ. I love him and he loves me more than I could ever fathom or understand. He offers salvation and mercy to all of us, and he teaches us how to love. Jesus loves us. He suffers with us and saves us. He walks beside us and shows us the way. Whatever you are going through, cling to him and he will see you through.

Jesus says in Matthew 11: 28-30, "Come to me, all you who labor and are burdened, and I will give you rest." I hope you find some encouragement, healing, wisdom, strength, and inspiration in the pages of this book. I pray that you continue to grow closer and closer to God, and that you find new opportunities every day to sow seeds of faith, hope, and love wherever you go.

Love,

Aaron

PART ONE: LETTERS OF ENCOURAGEMENT: You do not need to walk the journey alone.

FOR THE DAY YOU THINK YOU MIGHT BE GAY... BUT YOU'RE NOT SURE...

"Owe nothing to anyone, except to love one another; for the one who loves another has fulfilled the law. The commandments, "You shall not commit adultery; you shall not kill; you shall not steal; you shall not covet," and whatever other commandment there may be, are summed up in this saying, (namely) "You shall love your neighbor as yourself." Love does no evil to the neighbor; hence, love is the fulfillment of the law."

-Romans 13: 8-10

Dear Brother, Dear Sister, Dear Friend,

How are you feeling, right this moment, as you begin to read this letter? Perhaps you are a bit frightened, or absolutely terrified, or blissfully excited, or mildly curious. You might feel as if you are somehow crossing the threshold of a grand new adventure or preparing to confess some shameful secret. Were you recently surprised by an unexpected crush on a friend, classmate, or celebrity who shares your gender? Are you terrified, or exhilarated, by the thought that you might like boys, or girls, or people of diverse gender expressions, or all of the above? Have you found yourself daydreaming about what it would be like to hold hands with the guy on the math team, or the girl at the library who proofreads your essays, or the cute person who works the Saturday shift with you at the local diner? Have you gone to the movies and the park with a certain someone? Do you talk to them on the phone all night long, and do you share a kiss or two with them when no one is looking? Do you wonder what this is and what it means and what will happen next?

For a lot of us, it can be a challenge to understand and accept certain aspects of our sexualities. This deeply saddens me, because God made us as sexual beings and deems sexuality to be good. So why do some of us carry so much doubt and shame when it comes to embracing this element of who we are?

With tragic effectiveness and sometimes lethal consequences, some powers within our religious institutions teach us that love, and especially sexual love, is only good, holy, and pure when it is shared between a man and a woman. These messages are carried through thousands of mediums and voices, whether they be interpretations of Holy Scripture, religious textbooks, teachings from the pulpit, or direct and indirect comments made by pastors, mentors, family members, and friends. When feelings of longing, affection, or love grow in us for a person who shares our gender, or for someone who courageously defies gender norms, we are sometimes tempted to ignore, fight, hide, or deny them. We might try to convince ourselves that we can and should crush all desire that does not conform to our church's rules. In time, we might doubt that love, or at least earthly romantic love, could ever be ours.

And oftentimes, whether or not we attach shame to the thought of it, our sexual identities may simply be unclear. The path to self-discovery can be confusing and difficult to navigate. Am I gay? How do I know? Am I going through a phase? Am I having a crush that will come to nothing, fade, and mean little in the overarching story of my life? Am I having a one-time crush on the person I am meant to spend the rest of my life with? What does this all mean? Who am I?

There is so much good news I want to share with you. To begin, let me assure you that you do not need to figure it all out today. Life is a journey. Try to enjoy each step of it and learn as much as you can along the way. Enjoy a crush or a new friendship without trying to piece together overnight what it all means. You do not need to label yourself with any kind of identity unless you want to. It is enough to be in the moment, feel what you feel, and love who you love.

If you struggle with accepting that God will bless love between people of the same gender, believe me, I understand. For years, I believed that I had to be celibate forever unless I fell in love with a woman. My denomination taught me that experiencing same-sex attractions was an unfortunate and disordered condition. Growing up, I received many confusing and mixed messages. I was told that God loved me even if I was gay, but I was also told that I must stifle any romantic desire that would lead to intimacy with another man. I came to believe that love between people of the same sex was a sin. It felt like I had to continually kill certain parts of myself in order to be good enough for God's love, but those parts refused to die. I tried to give up my dreams of falling in love with a kind, beautiful man, but those forbidden hopes kept surfacing to torture me.

Years of prayer and Scripture study opened my heart to trust that wherever there is love, there is God. One scripture passage that transformed my heart was Romans 13: 8, which states, "Owe nothing to anyone, except to love one another; for the one who loves another has fulfilled the law." Before discovering this passage, I had spent years believing that God's law was a decree I needed to follow perfectly in order to earn my own salvation. In time, I learned this was merely foolishness and pride. I cannot save myself, and I need not try to do so, for I am saved by Christ. Jesus defeated sin and death on the cross. He is the fulfillment of the law, and our calling as Christians is to follow him. Any interpretations of moral commandments that compel us to reject love do not comply with the decree of Romans 13:8, which states simply and boldly that "the one who loves another has fulfilled the law."

I am not writing this letter to preach to you or convince you of any point of view. Rather, I am inviting you to open your heart to God, to cast all your fears and worries upon His loving care, and to seek the answers you yearn for in Him. I am a flawed and simple man, but He is the all-knowing, almighty, and all-loving Creator. Go to Him. Follow Him. Trust Him. Have faith that if you seek the way in and through Him, He will guide you. You never need to be afraid.

God knows us completely. Sometimes we feel as if we are drowning in the mysteries of our lives. Who am I? What am I doing here? What is my purpose, today? What is the purpose of my entire existence? Who will love me and who will I love? How do I love well?

When the search for answers becomes overwhelming, turn to the comforting wisdom of Psalm 139: 13-14: "You formed my inmost being; you knit me in my mother's womb. I praise you, so wonderfully you made me; wonderful are your works! My very self you knew." God created us and loves us unconditionally. People in committed relationships, including same-sex couples, bring love and life to each other and the world through the families they create together. Sexuality is a gift from God and therefore something to be thankful for and cherish. It is a glorious fire that touches many elements of our identities, but at the same time, we are more than our sexualities. Do not get so lost in romance and sex that you forget everything else.

The search for identity involves both discovering our true nature and making choices to determine who we shall become. Take time to explore your ancestors and imagine what their dreams were for you. Search for interests or causes that ignite your passions. Listen for an internal call to fight for some particular justice in your community and the world. Explore whatever brings forth your creativity, your kindness, your humor, your compassion. As you learn more deeply who you are, and as you choose more definitely the person you want to be, give thanks and praise to the God who made you, who sees you, and who loves you. Search for where you belong in this world, all the while knowing that you ultimately belong with the one true God, the one who holds you now and will hold you forever if you let Him.

And so, in the middle of all the questions, doubts, and fears about your sexual identity, remember that getting to know yourself completely is a lifelong journey that must be embarked upon anew every day. In this moment, let it be enough to know that you are a child of God. You are loved, cherished, and redeemed by the one who created and sustains all things. You are called to be a witness to God's unconditional love. You are born with gifts and talents that can help build up God's Kingdom, day by day. Over time, you will make courageous choices and cowardly ones, and good and bad events will happen that are outside your control. No matter what, God will meet you in your triumphs, your mistakes, and the quiet moments of everyday life. Through it all, at your core, you will remain a unique being fully known and loved by God.

Love,

Aaron

FOR THE DAY YOU WISH YOU WERE STRAIGHT

"Then Jesus came with them to a place called Gethsemane, and he said to his disciples, 'Sit here while I go over there and pray.' He took along Peter and the two sons of Zebedee, and began to feel sorrow and distress. Then he said to them, 'My soul is sorrowful even to death. Remain here and keep watch with me.' He advanced a little and fell prostrate in prayer, saying, 'My Father, if it is possible, let this cup pass from me; yet, not as I will, but as you will.'"

- Matthew 26: 36-39

Dear Sister, Dear Brother, Dear Friend,

Life can be difficult. I struggled with questions and doubts regarding my sexual orientation for years before admitting to myself that I was gay. As I grew closer to acknowledging the truth, I tried to tell myself that I was who I was, that God loved me no matter what, that I needed to accept my own nature.

One quiet, lonely night, as I lay in bed, the enormity of my situation struck me like a sudden storm. I felt irreparably broken, like the part of me that was meant for love had been permanently corrupted by disease and sin. All my life, I had dreamed of falling in love with a woman, making her my wife, and raising children that were born of our flesh becoming one. I had built so much romance and so much happiness into this dream. I wanted it desperately and there was no room for anything else. I did not believe such love was possible with another man. In fact, I was convinced that it would be morally reprehensible to even hope for such a thing. And so, as I lay there in the darkness, for the first time, I asked God to make me straight.

And yet, in that moment, the Spirit of God was with me. She reminded me of Christ's agony in the garden the night before his crucifixion, the night before he bore the weight of all sin and death for the salvation of humanity. As it is written in Matthew 26: 39: "He advanced a little and fell prostrate in prayer, saying, 'My Father, if it is possible, let this cup pass from me; yet, not as I will, but as you will.'"

My struggles are nowhere near those of Jesus. He is God incarnate as man, Love made flesh, the only one capable of reuniting fallen creation to our God. I am not so blind as to think my suffering equates with his. However, he took on human flesh to save us and to show us how to live. The night I wished to be made straight was my personal moment in Gethsemane. I could see before me the grief that my sexual orientation would bring to certain members of my family. I could see the loss of any hopes I might hold for one day loving a wife and biological children. I could see years of struggle as I sorted through what this undesired reality meant for me and my little corner of the world. I faced my moment on the cross, and I was given the grace to follow the example of my savior. I prayed to my God, "Not as I will, but as you will."

In this life, there will be crosses for all of us to bear. We face a constellation of adversities, temptations, vices, oppressors, and demons. Much of the world and, sadly, sometimes our dearest loved ones, will fall prey to certain falsehoods. In their ignorance, many will teach us there is something wrong with being gay. Many will lead us to believe in lies, to think that being different from the majority makes us damaged or less valuable. There is constant pressure to conform, to pretend to be something we are not. Too often we are led to believe that we need to find a way to be straight for our stories to have happy endings.

Listen to the words of Romans 8: 38-39: "For I am convinced that neither death, nor life, nor angels, nor principalities, nor present things, nor future things, nor powers, nor height, nor depth, nor any other creature will be able to separate us from the love of God in Christ Jesus our Lord." God creates each of us and embraces us with a love that is unstoppable. She walks with us as we grow into the people we choose to become, day by day. Being gay could never change that.

God made us gay for a purpose. As I lay in bed that night, praying to be straight, some part of me remembered to say, "Not as I will, but as you will." About a year later, I had an insight that God made me gay for a reason: there was a man out there who was lonely, who needed someone to hold him, who needed someone to love, who needed me. Dreaming of this man gave me the strength to stand firm in my God-given identity. Furthermore, being gay has deepened my capacity for mercy and opened my eyes to the suffering of others. Deep in my heart, I feel called to share the good news of God's unconditional love with people who are shunned by traditional religious institutions and society in general. My own life experience has prepared me for this mission, and I am grateful for the opportunity to serve God and Her people.

Being gay does not hold us back from our dreams. We can still dream of marriage and children. We can still dream of growing closer to God and deeper in Her love. We can still live in service to others. We can still explore the world, create art, play basketball, plant lilac bushes, swim in the ocean, hike in the rainforest, start a business, or spend a year traveling the country in a beat-up minivan. Life is full of opportunities. Some might try to tell you that it is impossible to find happiness, that you should give up, that being gay prevents you from finding joy, love, integrity, or faith. But those people are wrong.

Our God is a God of hope. She did not make us gay to watch us suffer or crush our dreams. I believe She made us gay to open our hearts deeper in the ways of love.

Before realizing I was gay, I thought I had all the answers. I had studied religion at school and I was well educated in the doctrines of Christianity. I thought I was wise, but I was hard-hearted. I did not really search for the truth in the gospel of Christ or in the Holy Spirit. Rather, I searched for truth in my own opinions, and I was unforgiving of anyone, including myself, who diverted from my own vision of right and wrong.

The spiritual journey I have undertaken in the light of my sexual orientation has deepened my compassion, my empathy, my humility, and my understanding of God's unconditional love and saving grace. I shudder to think of the person I would be if I were granted my wish that night and turned straight. I would never have learned to question my judgmental attitudes or the harshness I inflicted on myself and others.

And in being gay, I have discovered new and beautiful dreams that never would have been born if I were straight. I know the joy of breaking stereotypes simply by existing as both a proud gay man and faithful Christian. I have made phone calls and walked in marches advocating for marriage equality. I have spoken up for better services for young people experiencing homelessness, so many of whom identify as sexual minorities. One of the greatest joys of my life is volunteering with a youth group for lesbian, gay, bisexual, trans, questioning, and queer people in my home town. I learn so much from these young people about how to be a kind, loving, and courageous human being. I am so proud of everyone in my youth group, and I am so thankful to have them in my life. All of these experiences are dreams come true, and they only came to pass because I am gay.

Also, remember that many of our straight friends go through similar struggles. It helps to build bridges of understanding rather than walls that tear us apart. Being straight is not necessarily easy. Most of us, gay and straight and everyone in between, struggle to find a true sense of identity at some point in our lives. And most of us struggle to find friends who understand. Many of us search and search and search to find where we belong and what we were put on this earth to do. Changing one aspect of our identities would not take away these universal human challenges. In fact, we can bring meaning to our journeys by realizing that these shared struggles help us to connect with one another.

Hold on, my friend. You may be at a point in life where you wish you could be straight. You may face loneliness and your own fears as I did, or you might face more distressing external forces, such as violence or rejection at school or in your home. It is okay to wish you were straight sometimes. Feelings come and go, and they simply are what they are. But I implore you to search for reasons to be thankful for who you are. Be safe, and find people in your community who will help you see that you are created in the image of the almighty God who loves you. Consider reaching out to people you trust for support. Talk to someone about what you are going through— a teacher, a family member, a counselor, or a friend. God often shows Her love for us through the love of other people. If you can't think of someone you feel comfortable opening up to, there are many resources you can connect with through a simple phone call. For example, you can call The Trevor Project at 1-866-488-7386 twenty-four hours a day. The good people who answer the phones are trained specifically to work with young people who identify as lesbian, gay, bisexual, transgender, queer, or questioning.

I hope and pray that in time, you will come to know that the world is blessed because of who you are. Pray with me today that God will build within you an unshakable faith and lead you to the joy and purpose She has in store for your life.

I wish you peace and deep joy, now and always.

Love,

Aaron

FOR THE DAY YOU FEEL OVERWHELMED BY UNDESERVED GUILT AND SHAME

"For freedom Christ set us free; so stand firm and do not submit again to the yoke of slavery."

- Galatians 5: 1

Dear Brother, Dear Sister, Dear Friend,

Jesus said, "'...I am the gate. Whoever enters through me will be saved, and will come in and go out and find pasture. A thief comes only to steal and slaughter and destroy; I came so that they might have life and have it more abundantly'" (John 10: 9-10). Jesus made it clear that he came so that we might live in joy, be filled with his Spirit, and love one another in true freedom. Why do we allow guilt and shame to steal, slaughter, and destroy our peace?

Guilt can be healthy when it arises from something we have done that hurts God, others, or ourselves. In fact, guilt can be a productive force that moves us to repent, open ourselves to God's grace, and surrender our lives more deeply to God. This is the purpose of guilt. It is good to listen to one's conscience and rectify any instance when one has done something wrong or failed to do something good.

Yet oftentimes we hold onto guilt after God has forgiven us. We refuse to forgive ourselves. Even worse, sometimes we feel guilty or ashamed for things that are not bad at all.

As gay Christians, we are in great danger of developing a deep sense of internal shame. Many of us have been exposed to hurtful ideas that say being gay is a disorder. We are sometimes taught that it is sinful to desire affectionate and sexual union with another person of the same gender under any circumstances. These ideas can wreak havoc in our souls. Even if we reject them in our conscious minds, their shadows sometimes linger under the surface and impact our lives in unexpected ways. For example, have you ever been plagued by feelings of doubt after the first few dates with a nice guy or girl? Do you wonder how such a person could ever like you, or do you sabotage a budding relationship and pretend you do not like the other person because deep down you simply do not feel lovable? Do you find yourself being afraid to take risks, try out for that sport, audition for that play, or apply for that job or college, because you automatically think you will fail? Or do you always make sure you are the loudest, funniest person in the room because you are terrified someone might see how sad or lonely you really feel deep inside? These are all examples of how shame infiltrates our lives in subtle ways.

In addition, when we are led to believe that sex is always sinful, we might be tempted to give up altogether on sexual virtue and let our sexualities run rampant. If dedicated love with one person is deemed sinful, why not just let loose? Sometimes, after living with this mentality for a while, we wake up as if from a dream and realize our hearts are broken and we have broken countless other hearts. We have used people rather than truly loving them as fellow human beings created and cherished by God, and we have let others use us. We may confess these sins to God, but due to those lingering shadows of a deeper shame, we may not really forgive ourselves.

Guilt and shame touches so many layers of our lives. The way to overcome them is surprisingly simple: we must embrace the truth. God loves us and made us as we are in God's image. God is love and God is good. It is true, we are human and we are broken by sin. At times, we will fall. But God will always be there to pick us up. All we need to do is let Him heal us, for we are already saved in Christ. Jesus did not suffer and die on the cross to watch us wallow in guilt, shame, and misery. As it is written in Galatians 5: 1, "For freedom Christ set us free; so stand firm and do not submit again to the yoke of slavery."

Today, I beg you, make the courageous choice to love God, love others, and love yourself. As it is written in 1 John: 4: 18, "There is no fear in love, but perfect love drives out fear because fear has to do with punishment, and so one who fears is not yet perfect in love." Jesus died so that we can have abundant life in him. He cleanses us of our guilt and shame so that we can live and love freely in the light of his resurrection. We must trust in his goodness and his truth.

If you feel guilty, pray. Ask God for forgiveness and for the grace to forgive yourself. Ask God to move your conscience to act as He wills in your life. Ask for His guidance and when He gives it, trust Him.

And when you do things that you regret, try to put them in perspective. Are you as concerned about the millions of starving people in the world, the unjust wars, the horrible acts of violence, the thousands of children who die of preventable diseases, the evils of racism and sexism and ableism, as you are about your personal violations of chastity? Respect and love and virtues of all kinds are important, but we need to let God forgive us and we need to forgive ourselves so that we can focus our attention on the things that matter the most. Christ set us free so that we can work beside Him to build up the Kingdom of God. Please do not let your own guilt and shame hold you back from doing your part to bring justice and peace to our world. We need you.

There may never be a flashing neon sign or audible voice telling you the words you need to hear, but you will find the truth if you seek it. Pray. Read the Holy Scriptures. Talk with mentors and trusted friends. Meditate. Journal.

And listen, listen, always listen for the quiet, whispering voice of the Holy Spirit in your own heart. God's love and forgiveness will find you in a thousand places if you open your eyes to see and your ears to hear.

Life is short. Do not waste a moment dwelling in guilt and shame. Jesus suffered, died, and rose again to set you free. Embrace that freedom, and let God work within it to make you the person you are meant to be.

Love,

Aaron

FOR THE DAY YOU CONTEMPLATE COMING OUT

"… and you will know the truth, and the truth will set you free."
-John 8: 32

Dear Sister, Dear Brother, Dear Friend,

You stand on the precipice of an important choice, one that may seem exciting, or terrifying, or impossible. Maybe you have a crush on your same-gendered best friend, or maybe you know that you are gay or bi or trans, or maybe you are still searching for all the answers, or maybe you have decided that labels do not matter to you at all. Regardless of where you stand, you may feel ready to share something about yourself with a particular person, or the whole world, something that until now you have been holding inside.

It is courageous to testify to the truth, and it is a heavy burden to carry secrets. When we hold back pieces of ourselves, people cannot see or know who we truly are. Secrets build walls and make us feel as if we are living a lie. Jesus says in John 8: 32 that "…the truth will set you free."

Coming out, telling others the truth of who we are, is more than a personal victory or sacrifice. It moves others to encounter the reality of homosexuality and gender diversity, and it invites them to consider what it means to be gay. For better or worse, if you are out, then whatever you do and however you act expands what it means to be a gay person in the world today. If you stand firm in your faith, in your sexual orientation, and in your gender, if you live in God's grace, honesty, humility, and truth while boldly professing you are gay, you will be a powerful witness to the unconditional love of God. You will also help break down stereotypes that bind your brothers and sisters and friends. You will help others find the courage to be their true selves.

Yet testifying to the truth can be dangerous. People will sometimes use our vulnerabilities to hurt us. Many of us have lost friends or been rejected by loved ones when they learn that we are different from them. If this has happened to you, I am so sorry. I pray that you find comfort and peace, that they find mercy in their hearts and the will to change, and that you come to a place of forgiveness for the harm they have caused with their ignorance and hate.

Coming out can be good and powerful, but it is vital to be wise about timing and execution. It is not cowardice to remain in the closet if coming out could bring harm to yourself or others. The truth of your identity is precious and good. People do not have the right to any information if they would use it to hurt you. Jesus teaches us, "Do not give what is holy to dogs, or throw your pearls before swine, lest they trample them underfoot, and turn and tear you to pieces" (Matthew 7: 6).

I do not believe Jesus wants us to hold judgement, resentment, or hatred for anyone, but I do believe he wants us to live in love. At times, he may call us to risk our safety and sacrifice ourselves to witness to the truth, but other times he may call us to quietly survive until all is made right in time. Each of our lives is a story of God's saving love. When we face crossroads, we must turn to Her for direction. We must seek Her in prayer, in Scripture, and in conversation with trusted people who truly have our best interests at heart.

Are you thinking of coming out? How exciting! I want you to experience the joy and freedom of living in the truth, and I want you to be safe. Here are some questions to prayerfully consider:

-Why do you want to come out at this time? What are you hoping will happen?

-How would your coming out be a blessing for the people in your life and in your community?

-How do you think people will react if you come out? What would the best case scenario look like? What would the worst case scenario look like?

-Who can support you in coming out? Would it be helpful to have someone by your side when you come out to a particular person? Who would be your best advocate? Who would be the best peacemaker?

-Would coming out put you at risk for physical harm? Would coming out put you at risk of homelessness? Would coming out put you at risk of losing your source of income?

-If you need to stay in a safe place after coming out, where will you stay?

-What words are the Holy Spirit moving you to say, right here, right now, today?

-Whatever you choose to do, how can you offer this experience, and all its consequences, to God? How can you let God into this moment and all the moments of your life?

Ask these questions in prayer and talk through your answers with trusted friends. Knowing the answers will help you make your choices with confidence. It can also help to practice coming out with someone you trust. Ask them to act out best and worst case scenarios so that you can practice how you will respond. Once again, it can be helpful to have someone with you as you come out, and it can help to know where you will stay if things do not go well. If you are thinking about leaving home, or if you have already been kicked out, you can get help by calling the National Runaway Safeline at 1-800-621-4000.

The funny thing about coming out is that it does not happen just one time. Every new school, every new job, and every person you meet is a fresh opportunity to reveal your sexual orientation and gender identity... or not. The choice to come out should always be yours, though sometimes people take that choice away by making assumptions or spreading rumors.

It was difficult for me to come out for the first time. I had no one to talk to about it because no one knew yet. At the time, I was riddled with anxiety and confusion. I was twenty-one years old and until that moment, I had always assumed I was straight. Over several months, I came to realize I was deeply attracted to a man I worked with, but I had experienced crushes on girls in the past. All my life, I had deeply internalized beliefs that denigrated homosexuality. I was ashamed and afraid and I did not know what was happening to me.

I needed to talk to someone about what I was going through. My three sisters are my best friends, but I did not want to burden all of them with what felt like a heavy and painful secret. I decided to talk to my fellow middle sister, Kelly. We have always been close, and since middle school, we have gone for long walks while talking about books, life, politics, faith, and everything else. We left on one of our usual walks through the neighborhood one cold, dry night in early spring, and I told her that I thought I might be gay. Kelly was so shocked that she kind of collapsed onto a park bench and took a minute to breathe with her head between her knees. Both of us laughed nervously for a while. From the first moment, she listened endlessly and supported me through my journey of discovering who I was and who I was called to be. She helped me see over and over the need to give my life to God and trust that God would lead me where I needed to go.

It took three years of agonizing self-reflection before I felt ready to come out to my other sisters and my parents. During that time, I shared my internal struggle with a librarian friend, spiritual director, friend from church, and mentor at work. They were all dear people who loved me unconditionally and took the time to build trust with me so that I felt safe telling them what I was going through.

Throughout this period, I imagined my parents would have horrible reactions to my coming out. I knew my other sisters would fully support me, but I did not want them to feel like they had to lie to my parents, and I was not ready to share the truth with the world yet. I was still trying to figure it out for myself. To further complicate things, I lived with my parents during this period to save up money to pay off student loans. Years of confusion, anxiety, and fear led to a depression that I tried and failed to hide.

When I was settled with a job and apartment of my own, I finally came out to my parents and my other sisters. To my joyful surprise, my family was incredibly supportive. I had built up great fear that they might hate, judge, or reject me, but they told me they loved me, they supported me, and it would be okay. It was a pivotal moment in my life. I realized fear had been a vicious enemy that held me back from embracing the many blessings life held in store for me.

I came out in my mid-twenties when I was completely self-sufficient and established as an adult. It was destructive to hide my sexual orientation for years, yet I felt extremely safe and secure coming out because I was independent enough to care for myself no matter what happened. I also suspect certain members of my family were more compassionate with me because they had watched me struggling for years and could likely guess the cause. Would I change my coming out choices if I could? Would it have been better for me to talk with my family about my suspicions sooner? I do not know. I can only trust that it is what it is, and God has moved in my story to work love, trust, and reconciliation in my family. That is what matters.

If you are struggling with the choice of whether or not to come out, pray. Ask God to lead you and trust that She will. If you feel called to wait a while before you come out, pray for the patience and endurance to carry on, and pray for the wisdom to know when the time is right to speak the truth. If you feel called to come out now, pray for courage, the wisdom to know the words to say, and the strength to endure whatever comes your way.

We know that persecution is part of the Christian life because our Lord and Savior, Jesus Christ, was crucified for our salvation. As part of the Body of Christ alive in the world today, there will be times when we must share in his crucifixion. Yet we also know that Jesus rose from the grave and conquered sin and death forever. We must walk with him, die with him, and rise with him to be his disciples. In Matthew 5: 11-12, Jesus says, "Blessed are you when they insult you and persecute you and utter every kind of evil against you (falsely) because of me. Rejoice and be glad, for your reward will be great in heaven. Thus they persecuted the prophets who were before you." When we bear suffering in the name of truth and righteousness, we share in the mission of the prophets and the cross of Christ. We could not be in better company. Trust that God is with you in every trial. No matter what the world says, She made you as you are and calls you to Herself.

Be proud of who God made you to be, and be brave.

Love,

Aaron

FOR THE DAY YOU ARE REJECTED BY A LOVED ONE FOR BEING GAY

"I heard a loud voice from the throne, saying, 'Behold, God's dwelling is with the human race. He will dwell with them and they will be his people and God himself will always be with them as their God. He will wipe every tear from their eyes, and there shall be no more death or mourning, wailing or pain, for the old order has passed away.'"
- Revelation 21: 3-4

Dear Brother, Dear Sister, Dear Friend,

I am so sorry that this day has come to pass. Family and friends have a sacred duty to love one another. We are called to see, celebrate, and nurture the good in each other, to witness the image of God in each other's eyes. In his book *Works of Love*, philosopher Soren Kierkegaard (1962) demonstrates that Christians are called to love all their neighbors as themselves, and that this command from God extends to all people, not just the people who live or look or believe like we do. We are called even to love our enemies, for love alone is the fulfillment of the law of God.

Sadly, so many times, we all fall short of this great command to love our neighbors. We fail even to love those closest to us. And when we fail, people get hurt. Today is a day when others failed to show you the love you deserve, and I am sorry.

Maybe a parent told you there is something wrong with you, or maybe a friend told you they don't want to see you anymore, or maybe a pastor told you that what you feel inside is morally wrong. Whatever situation you find yourself in today, someone failed to see the good in you, and they chose to believe a lie.

It can be especially troubling if the person who hurt you professes to be a Christian. Their act of rejection may lead you to feel as if you are abandoned by all people of faith. Believe me when I say that being rejected for being gay is a flagrant violation of the way of Christ. In John 13: 34-35, Jesus says "… I give you a new commandment: love one another. As I have loved you, so you also should love one another. This is how all will know that you are my disciples, if you have love for one another."

Why did this person fail to love you perfectly today?

Human beings are complicated and flawed. We do not always see the truth. Sometimes we cling to hurtful ideas because they make us feel safe, powerful, or right. And sometimes we fail to open our hearts to the living truth of God, the radical truth of Love who became man and died on the cross for our salvation. Sometimes people believe things that are not true because they are too afraid to question, to grow, to change, to challenge. Fear is the enemy of love. It is a tragedy when people choose hate and fear over love, and it happens too often.

So what now? Where will you go from here? Please, in this moment of deep agony, pray. Lift your suffering and your rejection to God. Invite Him to work in your heart, in your relationships, in your struggles. Our Jesus faced the pain of rejection when he was abandoned by his friends and disciples the night before his death. They left him to face the torments of the cross alone. He understands what you are going through. He is with you. Go to him, talk to him, and listen for his voice. Let his compassion enter your soul and heal you.

Now is a dangerous time. Pain can easily turn into a poison that turns us away from God, kills our love, and buries us in hatred, judgment, and bitterness. It is so easy to hate and it can be so challenging to love. Please, do not let this primal wound steal your goodness, your innocence, or your truest self in Christ.

Someone hurt you today. It was wrong. It was evil at work. But please, let the evil stop with you. Let God transform your pain into an ocean of mercy. Remember those who suffer with you and remember that the person who hurt you also suffers. They committed an act of cruelty, cowardice, ignorance, injustice, and hate today. Sin like that is born of pain and it will breed deeper pain in their soul.

It would be so easy to hate the parent, the friend, the minister who rejected you. But hate only breeds more hate. Listen to the words of Jesus from Matthew 5: 44-45: "But I say to you, love your enemies, and pray for those who persecute you, that you may be children of your heavenly Father, for he makes his sun rise on the bad and the good, and causes rain to fall on the just and the unjust."

Invite God to move in you so that a miracle can happen. God calls us to love our enemies, but this does not mean that we should allow ourselves to be abused or remain in unhealthy situations. Jesus came so we could live in freedom, not subjugation. Indeed, Galatians 5: 1 reads, "For freedom Christ set us free; so stand firm and do not submit again to the yoke of slavery." It is sometimes necessary to remove ourselves from contact with people who hurt us in order to be safe, to be healthy, and to grow into the people God created us to be. But even if a relationship changes or ends, true freedom can only be achieved if we let go of hatred, malice, and bitterness. In our hearts, we must hope and pray for the redemption and salvation of those who hurt us. Would it not be a beautiful thing if they reformed and offered us love instead of hate? Would it not be miraculous if, one day, the parent, the friend, the pastor embraced you with kindness, mercy, and an open heart? Even if they were forever removed from your life, would it not be better for a quiet peace to lie between you rather than bitterness, anger, and unspoken pain?

The journey to inner peace and reconciliation is long and difficult, especially when the wounds we carry seem unforgiveable. I am not asking you to ignore your pain or hide it deep within yourself. I am not asking you to act the part of the perfect Christian. This would be dishonest, unhealthy, and hurtful for you and everyone around you. Such artifice would keep you from sharing your testimony about the deep pain of sin and the saving power of God's grace. It will take time for you to heal. You are hurting, and I am sorry. I simply hope that this pain moves you not to bitterness or hate, but instead ever closer to the heart of God.

God heals all our wounds and moves in us to bring about His Kingdom. We must hold onto each other in times of suffering. Reach out to good friends and family members you can trust. Let them hold you and care for you. Let the love of God shine through them into your soul. And together, let us dream of the day promised in Revelation 21: 3-4: "I heard a loud voice from the throne, saying, 'Behold, God's dwelling is with the human race. He will dwell with them and they will be his people and God himself will always be with them as their God. He will wipe every tear from their eyes, and there shall be no more death or mourning, wailing or pain, for the old order has passed away.'"

Until that perfect day of the new creation comes, we hold each other, and God holds us in the quiet. Someone failed to embrace you today, but please know that I embrace you, I accept you, and you belong with me, with the people of God, and with the human race. You are loved by me and you are loved by God. Let us work together to stretch the embrace wider, find the other people out there who are hurting with us, and let everyone in.

Love,

Aaron

PART TWO: LETTERS OF HEALING: Let God carry
you and make you whole again.

FOR THE DAY YOU FEEL UNLOVABLE

"He said to him, 'You shall love the Lord, your God, with all your heart, with all your soul, and with all your mind. This is the greatest and the first commandment. The second is like it: You shall love your neighbor as yourself. The whole law and the prophets depend on these two commandments.'"

-Matthew 22: 37-40

Dear Sister, Dear Brother, Dear Friend,

We were all created to love God, love each other, and love ourselves. The creation story in Genesis 1-2: 4 confirms that God looked over all of creation and "found it very good." Human beings were made in the very image and likeness of God. We derive our dignity and worth from our nature as children of the divine Creator.

We do not need to do anything to be worthy of love. And yet, many of us have a gaping wound that makes us feel like we are not good enough, beautiful enough, smart enough, funny enough, or deserving of anyone's time or affection. We sometimes feel we are not lovable. We wonder, how could someone want me, especially if they really saw how ugly I am on the inside? Or maybe we simply see ourselves as basic, bland, or empty. We think there is nothing special about us.

If you are reading this letter, it is because on some level, in some way, you feel unlovable, broken, unworthy, or unwanted. Maybe no one looks at you like you make their heart sing, or no one asks you how you're doing, or no one holds you when you break down. Maybe you are always left to cry alone. Maybe your dreams to find a friend or a lover or a sense of purpose have not yet come true, and it feels like they never will. Maybe you carry shame for who you are or guilt for what you have done, and you feel like redemption is forever beyond your reach.

I wish I could make your pain go away. I wish I could help you see the good in you, the courage, and the strength. I wish I could wrap you in a warm hug and tell you the words you so desperately need to hear.

But I cannot save you. I cannot convince you of your worthiness, your beauty, your dignity. By the grace of God, you have made it this far. I like the advice of counselors, popular icons, and spiritual people who tell us to make lists of our strengths, talk about our experiences with caring others, explore our feelings through art, and practice self-compassion. Yet I do not believe we can ultimately save ourselves. Rather, as followers of Jesus, our true path to healing lies in embracing the good news that God's love is for everyone. We were made to love God and our neighbors and even ourselves, for our Creator is a God of love.

We all carry wounds from the oppressive messages of the world, the damaging effects of sin, and the cruel experiences of our lives. These wounds sometimes generate a primal fear that we are inherently unlovable. How do we overcome this brokenness? We cannot do it alone. The truth is that only God can heal our wounds. She alone can convince us we our lovable because in Her, we can experience what it means to be truly and completely loved.

If we open ourselves to God, She will meet us in the darkness and fill us with Her presence. When we are united with God, the Spirit of love overflows from our hearts and works healing and salvation in the lives of others.

Listen carefully to the words of Jesus in Matthew 22: 37-40: "... 'You shall love the Lord, your God, with all your heart, with all your soul, and with all your mind. This is the greatest and the first commandment. The second is like it: You shall love your neighbor as yourself. The whole law and the prophets depend on these two commandments.'" God made us for love. First we must love God, for God is the source of everything. And then we are called to love our neighbors as ourselves, because we cannot truly love others unless we love ourselves, too.

The tragic secret is that when we dwell in our own misery and pain, we are emotionally paralyzed and spiritually blinded to the suffering of others. If we doubt our own goodness, we fail to see opportunities to connect and serve. Why would we subject other people to our presence if we think we are ugly, broken, unholy, and worthless? And so, believing all these lies, we ignore others, or push them away, or show them only fake, hollow, dead versions of ourselves because we are afraid to show them who we really are. Or worse, we are so blinded by misery and self-pity that we fail to even notice the suffering of others, or care about it, or seek opportunities to serve.

If we open our hearts to God, She will prove we are lovable by loving us. Her love is simultaneously awesome and gentle. It cannot be denied or stopped unless we refuse it, because God would never force Herself on anyone.

You can experience God's love anywhere and at all times. Pray and ask God to be with you, to hold you, to love you. Search for God's voice speaking to you in songs, in poetry, in books, in films. Read the Scriptures and listen for the tenderness and mercy of God's love for you in the moments of your daily life. Open your eyes to beauty in nature, in art, in whatever inspires passion in your heart, and see in that beauty God's many blessings for us all. In the suffering of your life, open yourself to God's presence. Allow God to guide you and hold you in your sorrow.

One of the best ways to share in God's love is through loving other people. God brings us together in many ways. Through loving each other, we love God. As it is written in 1 John 4: 7-8, "Beloved, let us love one another, because love is of God; everyone who loves is begotten by God and knows God. Whoever is without love does not know God, for God is love." God puts people in our lives and calls us to love the people we meet in different ways. Sometimes we yearn for a certain kind of love that is not yet ours. We may yearn for the kiss of a boyfriend or girlfriend when we are single, or we may yearn for a kind word from the parent we never knew, or we may hope for just one friend to walk down the hallway beside us. As young gay people, we are often minorities in our schools, workplaces, hometowns, or faith communities, and this sometimes makes it harder to find someone to fall in love with or a friend who understands implicitly what we are going through. It might also lead to moments of painful rejection or misunderstanding with people we care about.

It can be heartbreaking to yearn for a kind of love that is not yet ours, and it can be easy to see this absence as proof that we are unlovable. For years, I believed deep down that being single meant that I was not good enough and that no one would ever want me. Eventually, I learned that whenever I felt this way, I should pray the words, "God, please help me to love the people in my life today." When I offer this request to God, my eyes are opened to family members, friends, co-workers, neighbors, and strangers on the street who I can love with kind words, practical gifts, meaningful conversations, quality time, or humble acts of service. We need to have faith that God loves us and calls us to love one another. This faith is all the proof we need to trust that we are lovable.

I cannot do anything on my own, and I often fall short of being the man I could be. But God is always there to lift me up after I fall. She always helps me get out of the messes I make. She loves me, and even in my moments of exhaustion, sorrow, or rage, Her love calls me to be more and more like Her.

Do not believe the lie that you are unlovable. You were loved from the moment of your conception and you are chosen for good works and blessings by our Lord. As it says in 1 Corinthians 12: 27, "Now you are Christ's body, and individually parts of it." We have been given the sacred honor and responsibility of being the hands and feet of Christ in the world today. We are his Body and he lives in us. We are each given unique gifts to be used for building up the Kingdom of God, establishing justice, and spreading the good news of salvation to all the world. Let us not waste time dwelling on our failures and imperfections. Let us instead embrace the new life given to us in Christ.

You are loved, and if you invite Her to do so, God will show you how to share that love with others. She will guide you. Whatever happens, God will be with you, and there's nothing better in all the world than spending time basking in the love of God.

Love,

Aaron

FOR THE DAY YOU FEEL ALONE

"Go, therefore, and make disciples of all nations, baptizing them in the name of the Father, and of the Son, and of the holy Spirit, teaching them to observe all that I have commanded you. And behold, I am with you always, until the end of the age."'

\- Matthew 28: 19-20

Dear Brother, Dear Sister, Dear Friend,

It breaks my heart that today you feel alone. We all have moments where a sense of isolation and disconnection sinks to our very bones. We might find ourselves in a new home or new town or new school where we do not know anyone. Or someone, a parent, a lover, a friend may walk out the door and abandon us when we need them most. Or we may be surrounded by people who care about us and yet, for some reason we may not understand, we still feel invisible. We can feel alone in our own homes, and we can suddenly find ourselves without a home at all.

Sometimes it feels impossible to find people to connect with. Many of us struggle with feelings of anxiety, self-doubt, or self-loathing. All this negativity can make it feel impossible to put ourselves out there. It becomes easy to believe that no one will ever like us or even want to talk to us, and we give up before we even get started. Such feelings are often rooted in experiences of being rejected or bullied. If people have hurt us in the past, it is very difficult to trust anyone. It is easier to build up walls to protect ourselves, even though this leaves us alone.

But maybe you struggle in a different way. Maybe you are well-liked and have lots of friends to spend time with, but you feel inauthentic. Maybe you feel like you wear a mask of charm, charisma, sugary sweetness, toughness, snarkiness, or whatever it is you think people want to see. Deep down, you know this false image keeps others from seeing the real you, and this makes you feel like no one really knows you. You can have legions of friends and still feel alone.

Maybe you have become someone you do not really like in order to belong. Maybe you find yourself gossiping about others, being mean, spending too much money, using drugs or alcohol, having sex without love or meaning, or wasting your time on things you do not care about because you want to fit in with a culture that tells you these are the things you are supposed to do. You wanted to be part of the crowd, and now here you are, but you know in your soul this is not the person you were made to be, and this is not the person you want to be.

Or maybe you are angry at the whole world, and you do everything you can to push people away. Maybe you are so hurt from the past and so afraid of experiencing more pain that you convince yourself you are better, smarter, or more righteous than others. You cut them all out of your heart. You give up on relationships because it feels easier to keep people at a distance through harsh judgement than to connect with people who are flawed.

Or maybe you feel solid in who you are and you like yourself just fine, but you have trouble finding people who are like you. You do not always feel easy around people and yearn to find others who share some of your identities, experiences, beliefs, or interests. Yet they remain hard to find.

We were created to love and to be loved. There is a yearning in our souls to connect with God and with other people. At the moment of our creation, Genesis 2: 18 tells us that, "The LORD God said: 'It is not good for the man to be alone. I will make a suitable partner for him.'" Suffering comes when sin, misunderstandings, hatred, prejudice, and lies tear us apart from one another and from God. I wish I could spare you from the pain of loneliness, but yearning for connection is a part of our human condition. In our world, which is broken by sin, there will be times when we feel the weight of loneliness.

When Jesus took on flesh, he shared in all aspects of our humanity except committing sin. He understands us because he experienced profound loneliness at times. In fact, he teaches us that walking the lonely, homeless road is sometimes a part of being his disciple. Luke 9: 57-58 says, "As they were proceeding on their journey someone said to him, 'I will follow you wherever you go.' Jesus answered him, 'Foxes have dens and birds of the sky have nests, but the Son of Man has nowhere to rest his head.'" This verse breaks my heart because it opens my eyes to the painful loneliness experienced by Jesus. Every sin throughout the ages is a rejection of God's love, and Jesus feels each violation of love personally. Knowing this calls me to open my life to Jesus so that he might finally have a place to abide on earth, and that place is within my own heart.

We all experience loneliness and isolation as a result of sin, but through God's saving grace, we are reconciled to God and to each other. This is the joy of the gospel! Our calling as Christians is to live this truth at all times and in all circumstances. We must let God work in and through us to right wrongs, establish justice, and rekindle love until the fullness of the Kingdom of God is revealed at the end of time.

How would that look in your life? As you struggle with feeling alone in your own corner of the world, where is God calling you to seek love with Him and with other people?

It is such a blessing to find a friend, a family member, a lover who sees and cherishes you as you are. Love inspires us to grow into the people we are meant to be. Never give up the search. There are so many good and loving people out there who are looking for a person like you. Go find them. Be the friend they need.

How can you find someone to help soothe your loneliness? Start by living a full life today. Spend some time doing what you like to do. Take classes, join teams, or start a book club at the library. Go to concerts or dances. If you cannot afford them, see if you can work part-time at a music venue. Volunteer for causes you care about. Participate in community groups or service projects with your faith community. If they do not have what you are looking for, offer to lead something new. Even if you can't think of anything that sounds interesting or fun, put yourself out there and try something random. In time, you might discover interests and make friends in the most unexpected places. But try not to approach activities with great expectations that you will find a new best friend or someone to date right away. Rather, just put yourself places where you want to be and open your heart to love any neighbor who happens to show up.

When I was in my late teens and early twenties, I felt very much alone. I had dear family members in my life who loved me and whom I loved, but I felt like I needed friends of my own. I wanted to connect with people who understood what was happening in my life at that time, who shared my interests and beliefs and were going through what I was going through. Sadly, I let my desire for this specific kind of friend blind me to the good people who were right in front of me all along.

After graduating from college, I worked as a preschool teacher. I loved playing with the kids, reading books out loud, and belting out silly songs to make the little ones laugh. Yet every day was an exhausting challenge. One of the people who helped me through was my co-teacher, Janet. This eighty-year old, spit-fire, fearless woman had raised nine children and taught for decades. She had a side-splitting, irreverent sense of humor and was not afraid to boss me around, which I needed now and then. Janet was very different from the young-Christian-gay-male buddy I had been praying for, but her friendship rapidly became one of the greatest blessings of my life. To this day, she makes me laugh, listens, reminds me to be brave, and gives me great advice. Janet grew up during the Great Depression and she is one of the strongest people I know. Through her, I discovered that I can find amazing people to connect with who are different than me, and that is a wonderful thing! I do not need to find friends who are exactly like me. I simply need good people to love who love me back.

Maybe you have good and loving friends and family, but there is a special ache in your heart to find romantic love. This particular kind of loneliness can be painful. Pray about it. If this longing for love was placed in your heart by God, trust that God will guide you to your soul mate at the right time. Psalm 37: 4 states, "Find your delight in the LORD who will give you your heart's desire." I do not think this means God will give us whatever we want. Rather, I believe it means if we truly give our lives to God, He will give us the desires that will lead us to true meaning and happiness. After discerning what God wants for us, we can trust in the words that Jesus speaks in Luke 11: 9-13: "And I tell you, ask and you will receive; seek and you will find; knock and the door will be opened to you. For everyone who asks, receives; and the one who seeks, finds; and to the one who knocks, the door will be opened. What father among you would hand his son a snake when he asks for a fish? Or hand him a scorpion when he asks for an egg?"

Searching for a soul mate has been a struggle for me. I definitely had a late start. I did not realize I was gay until I was twenty-one years old. At that time, I developed a crush on a friendly, adorable co-worker. I did not know what my own feelings meant at first. Was I gay? Was I bi? Was I having a hormonal episode that would pass? Back then, I did not believe it was ever morally right for two men to love each other in a romantic, sexual way. And yet, here in my heart was this longing. All my life, I had always dreamed about falling in love with a woman and building a family with her. Feeling attracted to another man was a complete and total shock.

After a day or two of painful confusion, I sat on the bus and opened my heart to God in prayer. I imagined Jesus watching me with kind eyes, and I said to him, "Jesus, I give you my heart. You can keep it for yourself alone, or you can share it with the person I'm meant to be with. I trust you." This prayer brought me great peace in those early days of confusion and questioning.

I wish I could say I always remain in a stance of blissful surrender to God, but that would be a terrible lie. The first man I had a crush on ended up being straight, and that was a painful disappointment. I wrestled for years with deeply ingrained homophobic beliefs and eventually came to the conclusion that God is love and, therefore, if true love exists between any two people, God is there. When I first decided to give dating a try, I experienced some false starts and early disappointments. I made mistakes. I started thinking I could not be happy or fulfilled until I found my perfect match. Dating became all about me. Rather than turning to God's mercy and holding onto hope, I allowed myself to grow bitter and despairing. I kept dating, but over time, I realized I was not even looking for love anymore because I did not believe that love was real. I was only using people to ease the pain of loneliness. Some of those people really liked me, and I ended up hurting them.

This painful discovery forced me to step back and reflect on my dating life. I realized that the idea of love with a romantic partner had become a false idol for me. Rather than opening my heart to love and letting God guide me, I attempted again and again to find happiness and satisfaction in the arms of another man. We experience God's love through the love of others, but I had lost sight of the truth that love comes first and foremost from God. I now realize that I must continually smash the idol and remember the prayer I made on the bus in those early days of questioning my sexuality: "Jesus, I give you my heart. You can keep it for yourself alone, or you can share it with the person I'm meant to be with. I trust you."

Jesus is there to take me back every time.

If you are yearning for romantic love, pray about it. Ask God to help you grow into the person you need to be for your soul mate. Open your heart to the people in your life today. Love your family, friends, neighbors, and even your enemies. Let God guide you each step of the way. Trust Him. I talked to my priest once about feeling lonely and wondering whether or not I would ever find anyone to marry. He listened, gave me a warm, knowing smile, and said, "You'll find each other."

Remember, the truth is that we are never alone because God is always with us. He is always here to love us, hold us, walk beside us, and show us the way. As Jesus sends his followers, including us, out into the world, he says, "Go, therefore, and make disciples of all nations, baptizing them in the name of the Father, and of the Son, and of the holy Spirit, teaching them to observe all that I have commanded you. And behold, I am with you always, until the end of the age'" (Matthew 28: 19-20).

This mission gives us the grace to know that whenever we encounter another soul, we encounter a neighbor who we are called to love as ourselves. It can be very difficult to find a best friend or the love of your life, but it is rarely a challenge to find a neighbor. God calls us to love the people around us, the strangers on the other side of the world, and even our enemies just as much as we love our dearest friends. And so the opportunity to love, to not be alone, is everywhere. You can always offer a caring hand or an encouraging word to everyone you encounter. Whether or not they take it is up to them.

So as you go through this season of solitude, I invite you to open your eyes and heart to God's presence. Cling to Him, let His love wash over you, and let the Spirit move within you. Let God's love generate new life in you and prepare you for connection with whoever you encounter. Do what you can to change the world for the better, and let go of everything else. God loves us as we are and, if we let Him, He will guide us to where we need to be.

Love,

Aaron

FOR THE DAY YOU REALIZE YOU HATE YOURSELF

"For we are his handiwork, created in Christ Jesus for the good works that God has prepared in advance, that we should live in them."

- Ephesians 2: 10

Dear Sister, Dear Brother, Dear Friend,

I know from personal experience that self-hatred can be a sly and nasty demon. Sometimes it feels like the world is training us to hate ourselves. Every image, every message, every story seems to whisper in our ears that there is something ugly with our faces, flawed with our bodies, embarrassing about our voices, shameful about our beliefs, or cowardly about how we live. Even our own thoughts mock and ridicule us. It becomes easy to obsess over and magnify our faults until the people we see in the mirror look like monsters.

Sometimes we hate ourselves for not being attractive enough, experienced enough, or confident enough. Sometimes we hate ourselves for being selfish and sinful. Sometimes we hate ourselves because we feel we have been permanently damaged and defiled by horrible things that were done to us in the past. Sometimes, if we are honest, we hate ourselves for being gay. We may not want to feel this way, but at times we crave to eradicate those sexual feelings that, so far, have brought nothing but frustration and inner turmoil.

As gay Christians, we are taught to carry a great deal of shame. Some of our preachers, families, and church doctrines have instructed us to believe that our natural impulses to love are disordered and sinful. We are sometimes taught to believe that this essential part of ourselves is bad, and so it becomes easy to hate ourselves to the very core.

As humans, we all make mistakes. It becomes easy to see our missteps as proof that we are unworthy of love. Sometimes we might even feel a twisted sort of satisfaction in self-hatred as if we are punishing ourselves justly for the evil we have done. But does this self-loathing make us better people? Does hating ourselves bring us closer to the purpose for which we were created? Does it bring us closer to God, to our neighbor, to service, to love?

Self-hatred does not yield greater love. It is exhausting. It drains our energy and leaves us empty. Even worse, we sometimes seek to chase self-hatred away through bouts of anger or violence. Whether we lash out at ourselves or others, bringing more hurt and pain into the world violates our mission as followers of Christ.

Hate is planted in us by thousands of voices that tell us we are not good as we are, that our mistakes cannot be forgiven, that our dreams are foolish and unobtainable, that our lives do not matter.

But these voices tell us lies. God created us. God loves us. God redeems us. She shaped us into who we are and walks beside us in every moment of every day. She knows everything about us and forgives us when we fail to be the people we were created to be. God is a parent who loves us unconditionally. As God says through Her prophet in Isaiah 49: 15, "Can a mother forget her infant, be without tenderness for the child of her womb? Even should she forget, I will never forget you."

If we are going to work beside our Lord to build up the Kingdom of God, we need to love ourselves. Remember what Christ teaches us about the greatest commandments in Mark 12: 29-31: "Jesus replied, 'The first is this: 'Hear, O Israel! The Lord our God is Lord alone! You shall love the Lord your God with all your heart, with all your soul, with all your mind, and with all your strength.' The second is this: 'You shall love your neighbor as yourself.' There is no other commandment greater than these.'" As human beings and children of God, we are all worthy of love and respect. If we exclude ourselves from love, we deny that love itself is a universal right endowed by God. She commands us to love ourselves not only for our own sake, but also so that we can fully love others with free and unbound hearts.

I was swallowed in a deep self-loathing for years. During that difficult time, I would go on long walks around town and pick at my psychological wounds with negative thoughts. I spent hours dwelling on everything that was wrong with me, every sin I had committed, and every good thing I had failed to do with my life. This took up so much time and energy that I was completely unaware of opportunities for love and service. How could I notice when a friend, classmate, or co-worker needed to talk if I did not have the energy to listen? How could I lead a service project when I was too filled with self-doubt to believe that anything I did mattered? I locked myself away from the world because I thought I was not good at anything. Throughout that time, the strengths placed in me by God were not allowed to bear fruit. I was trapped by a painful form of narcissism that put me and my misery at the center of everything instead of God. My self-hatred became my prison. How many good works were left undone while I remained blinded by my own self-hate? And all the while, I had little joy to share with the world because my heart and my mind were filled with spiritual poison. I had lost sight of the truth contained in Ephesians 2: 10: "For we are his handiwork, created in Christ Jesus for the good works that God has prepared in advance, that we should live in them."

Though it was hard to notice in the middle of it, I now see that I was blessed with boundless love through this difficult time. My parents, sisters, a few good friends, people from church, kind co-workers, inspirational music, and powerful books all found me at the right time and gave me the words, comfort, and support I needed. Eventually, God moved my heart and helped me to see where I had fallen. I started working with a counselor, identified patterns of negative thinking, and talked about painful experiences that led me to hate myself. I began challenging lies with the truth that God loves me and made me for love. The words of Ephesians 4: 4-5 came to life in my soul: "But God, who is rich in mercy, because of the great love he had for us, even when we were dead in our transgressions, brought us to life with Christ (by grace you have been saved)."

In a new and powerful way, I came to know deep within my heart that I am saved by Christ. Of course, I am not perfect. I continue to fall into emotional pitfalls and make mistakes. But that does not really matter. The important truth is that I earnestly desire to return my life to God, and so She lifts me up whenever I fall, again and again. My mission is not to be perfect, but rather to love God, follow Her, and to do Her will to the best of my ability. My heart sings thanksgiving and praise for my life, for my blessings, for my talents, and for the countless opportunities God gives me to participate in Her ongoing work of redemption. When I surrender myself to God's amazing love, it consumes me and there is no longer room to hate anyone, not even myself.

We need to overcome self-hatred and live in God's love. But how do we do that? How do we overcome a demon who has grown so strong and so deeply ingrained in how we view ourselves and our lives?

The way to start is by giving it all to God. Pray. Ask God to help you feel Her presence within you. Meditate on the words of 1 Corinthians 6: 19: "Do you not know that your body is a temple of the holy Spirit within you, whom you have from God, and that you are not your own?" Indeed, we are all temples of the Holy Spirit. We are places where God, who is love, chooses to dwell. God brings Her love into the world through us. We belong to Her. Ask God to heal your broken heart and give you eyes to see the strengths that She planted within you. Ask God to guide you in developing these strengths so that you can use them with others to build up God's kingdom of righteousness, justice, and truth.

Through prayer, explore good things about yourself. What do you like about how you look, how you act, how you live, what you believe, and who you are? Some of us find it challenging to think about good things about ourselves, but we need to push through any resistance. Naming our strengths gives glory to the God who created us. When we open our eyes to God's blessings, we grow in gratitude to God, love ourselves more deeply, and deepen our capacity to love others.

Another important way to overcome self-hate is to start enjoying your life. Explore nature, art, books, sports, poetry, or music that makes your happy. Find someone kind, smart, and beautiful and ask them to hang out some time. If they say no, find someone else and try again. Eat delicious food. Practice yoga. Write a story. Do what you love and thank God for the ability and opportunity to do it. Find the things that make you excited to be alive. Love your body not because of the way it looks but because of what you can do as a person with flesh. If you can jump, jump. If you can sing, sing. If you can dance, dance. If your body is impacted by a disability, you have a special opportunity to find new ways for the human body to move and navigate the world. You have much to teach others. I am convinced that disability, like a minority sexual orientation or gender identity, refers to a difference and not a problem. We must use what we have with joy rather than dwell too long in what we cannot do. In the words of writer and social justice advocate Helen Keller, "One can never consent to creep when one feels an impulse to soar" (Fuller, 1905, p. 9).

When you feel ready, take a look at the wounds in your past that might encourage you to hate yourself. It can help to do this work with a therapist, a pastor trained in mental health counseling, a trusted friend, or loving family member. In your conversations with a caring person and with God, review the traumas and lies that hurt you. Meditate on memories of the bully who split your lip or your spirit, the friend who abandoned you, the parent who told you it was wrong for two boys or two girls to love each other, the man who touched you. Offer your pain up to God and ask Her to bring healing and redemption to your life.

Ask God to help you make meaning of all you have been through. How have these experiences prepared you to be of greater service to others? How have they deepened your compassion and your understanding of God's grace? Can your pain move you to be a more loving and compassionate friend, brother, sister, child, parent, neighbor, or disciple of Jesus? Does thinking about your past make you angry with God, or doubtful of Her goodness? Pray about those feelings. It makes perfect sense to be angry and distrusting after experiencing suffering and injustice. God can handle your questions, your anger, and your doubts. God yearns for you to come to Her with every burden you carry. In time, I trust that She will give you the answers you seek, and your story will be a great testimony about the saving power of God.

Whoever you are, wherever you live, and whatever you have done, I want you to know that you are loved. God loves you, and I love you. You are cherished and you are precious. There is light in your eyes and good work before you. Please do not give up. Jesus is beside you in the struggle every step of the way. The ultimate victory has already been won through his death and resurrection. Let his love and grace wash over you. I hope that someday, little by little, you can learn to love yourself, too.

Love,

Aaron

FOR THE DAY YOU REALIZE YOU HATE THE ENTIRE WORLD AND DECIDE THAT NO ONE IS WORTH SAVING

"Love is patient, love is kind. It is not jealous, love is not pompous, it is not inflated, it is not rude, it does not seek its own interests, it is not quick-tempered, it does not brood over injury, it does not rejoice over wrongdoing but rejoices with the truth. It bears all things, believes all things, hopes all things, endures all things. Love never fails..."
-1 Corinthians 13: 4-8

Dear Brother, Dear Sister, Dear Friend,

There are days when we are so overcome with rage, pain, or despair that we cannot see any good in anyone. Maybe the people you share your life with have betrayed you. Maybe strangers look right through you. Maybe it feels as if everyone is out to hurt you or so wrapped up in themselves that they see nothing else. Sometimes the earth itself seems like a dead husk, a barren rock devoid of value or beauty.

Evidence of sin and the cruelty of fallen humanity lurks all around us. It can be hard to see beyond war, slavery, exploitation, selfishness, broken relationships, abuse, deceit, poverty, and pain. We live in a world where young people are kicked out of their homes or run away to escape abuse, and they often find themselves selling sex just to survive. And we live in a world where grown-ups pay to have sex with children. It sometimes seems like this planet and its people are too broken to be fixed and too lost to be found. Even if redemption were possible, it can feel like there is not one person alive worth saving.

I am so sorry that you have come to a moment of profound despair. There is so much horror in our world, and sometimes it overwhelms us. I have endured and witnessed far too many tragedies in my own life. I cannot tell you how many children I know who have been killed by drunk drivers. I used to work as a counselor with young people who survived tragic abuse. One twelve-year-old boy I worked with had been forced to endure years of sexual assault perpetrated by his mother's narcotics dealer. The mother had no money, so she traded her son's body in exchange for drugs. As I watched the young boy explode in anger over and over again, it became more and more difficult to believe that I could do anything to help him. I felt powerless. There were moments when it was easier to despair than to hope.

As gay Christians, we might sometimes find ourselves feeling outcast from both Christian and gay communities. We might feel like we do not belong anywhere, and the pain of this rejection can easily turn into an icy hate for the entire world. Sometimes we give up on the entire human race because our hearts are broken by a family member, friend, or lover. A special someone leaves us or refuses to love us back, and we shatter inside. Sometimes we are so exhausted from trying to survive that the little annoying things about our neighbors make us hate them. That person's shrill voice or that other person's know-it-all attitude or that one person's snide comments suddenly become a reason to despise them entirely. Sometimes we secretly hate ourselves, but we hide this unpleasant fact by projecting that hate onto the world.

It can be so easy to abandon our hopes, dreams, and ideals. It can be easy to use people for sex because we no longer believe in real loving relationships. It can be easy to say cruel things because cutting other people out of a group makes us feel like we belong with the crowd. It can be easy to ignore the homeless person on the street because everyone else does. If we find ourselves to be a homeless person on the street, it can be easy to hate the people who ignore us. It can be easy to get so wrapped up in our own feelings, technology, dreams, or desires that we ignore suffering, corruption, environmental destruction, and injustice.

But God calls us to rise above what is easy or expected. God calls us to be faithful to the gospel. As St. Paul says in Galatians 2: 20, "…yet I live, no longer I, but Christ lives in me; insofar as I now live in the flesh, I live by faith in the Son of God who has loved me and given himself up for me." When we open our hearts to God and allow God, who is love, to live in and through us, we no longer look for validation or peace from the world. We decide to give everything we have even when we receive nothing at all. We decide to forgive even when we are judged and hated. We look for goodness and potential in every soul. We strive to love unconditionally because God loves unconditionally. When we live this way, Jesus works through us. We need to have faith. Even when we fail to see positive results, our efforts matter. All we can do is partner together with Christ to build up the Kingdom of God.

When we allow ourselves to be embittered by anger and despair, we become blind to God's presence in our world, in each other, and in ourselves. We lose our connection with the sacred presence of the Holy Spirit who lives in every soul and every corner of creation. We lose sight of God's saving love, which offers redemption to all regardless of whether or not they deserve it.

Jesus bore all our pain and brokenness on the cross. He conquered sin and death through his resurrection. He stared deeply into the horror and the misery of life, and he overcame it. By opening ourselves to him, we can overcome it, too. As Jesus says in John 12: 24, "Amen, amen, I say to you, unless a grain of wheat falls to the ground and dies, it remains just a grain of wheat; but if it dies, it produces much fruit." We must die to ourselves, we must die to anger and bitterness and hate, so that we may rise with Christ into fullness of life.

If you find yourself hating the world and its people, please reach out for help. Talk to trusted family members, friends, and mentors about how you feel. Ask them to pray with you and for you. Ask them how they maintain hope, joy, and love in a broken world. Consider reaching out to a counselor. Sometimes, we hate the world because deep down, we hate ourselves.

If we give up in despair or bitterness, we cut God out of our lives, and we damn ourselves to misery. For years, I woke up every morning, forced myself out of bed, dragged my heavy body to the bathroom mirror, looked myself in the eye, and said, "Only a few more decades of this and then you get to die." I felt like every day was a battle, and I kept losing. On the outside, I put on a happy smile, worked for the causes I believed in deep down underneath it all, and studied hard in school. But inside I felt like everything I did was worthless. I started seeing everyone and everything around me through the same gloomy lens. I trusted in God, but I gave up faith that human beings could ever be trustworthy, faithful, or good. I gave up believing people could change. And I believed the lie that flaws made human beings unworthy of love. I hated the world for not being what I wanted it to be. I hated people, including myself, for not being perfect. Looking back, I realize that underlying my negativity was deeply rooted shame and self-hatred. I hated my sexuality and wished I could be straight. I could do nothing about who I was, and so I directed my rage at everything else. Needless to say, all of this anger and hate kept me from fully experiencing the loving grace of God, and I was therefore incapable of embracing the good work He was calling me to do.

Healing from all of this was a long journey marked by grace. I met with a counselor and discussed issues from my past. I spoke with family members, friends, and mentors who shared their struggles and insights with me. I kept lists of bits of wisdom I gained from people, books, and songs. I realized that God was leading me to the truth in a million ways, and all I had to do was open my eyes.

And so, we come to these important questions: How can we maintain love for a world that can be so cruel? How can we love those who hurt us and hurt others?

If you are struggling to find love in your heart for anyone or anything, please go to God in prayer. Let God know how you feel and ask Him to move within your soul. As you read Scripture and go to church, ask the Holy Spirit to give you new life. As is written in Psalm 119: 105, "Your word is a lamp for my feet, a light for my path."

When we are tempted to curse the world and our neighbors, we must remind ourselves that God calls us to radical mercy. Through the loving grace of Jesus' sacrifice, we are called to love everyone, including those who hurt and reject us. As Jesus says in Matthew 5: 44-45, "But I say to you, love your enemies, and pray for those who persecute you, that you may be children of your heavenly Father, for he makes his sun rise on the bad and the good, and causes rain to fall on the just and the unjust." We cannot live out this kind of love by our own power. Rather, we must invite God to live in us. We must allow God's infinite, unconditional, and healing love to grow in our hearts.

If you feel exhausted and loving others seems impossible, I invite you to search for one good memory, one moment in your past, when life felt right, good, and worthwhile. Find such a memory and hold onto it as evidence of God's loving presence. Let this moment in time be a promise for good things yet to come.

I hold onto a precious moment that happened when I was nine-years-old. My youngest sister, Molly, had been born a couple days earlier and was newly home from the hospital. I sat holding her and watched her sleep as her little fingers wrapped around mine. Her head, with its feathery light-brown hair, nestled perfectly in the crook of my arm. Her tiny chest rose and fell as she slept. I sat there with her for hours, held her, and watched her sleep. Molly was safe in my arms and I loved her. We were together and nothing else seemed to matter very much. My mom kept an eye on us as she went about doing various chores and things, and at some point, she came up to me and said,

"Aaron, you'll make a great dad someday." Those words planted a seed for one of the great dreams of my life, which is to be a father. I will never forget that moment as long as I live, and thinking about it always brings me joy.

When I encounter deep cruelty, when I feel powerless, when my heart is broken, when people spit on me or my beliefs, when people try to crush my dreams, when I start to think that this world and its people are not worth saving, I go back to that moment with my little sister. I remember how love for her consumed me and how, for a moment, the world became alive with joy. I remind myself that I am still living on the same planet where Molly was born and where she continues to live. This is the world that God made, and this is my time to be alive in it. I open my heart to God and ask Him to show me how I am called to love today.

Sometimes it is difficult to escape feelings of despair, hopelessness, or hate. It is then that we realize most fully that love is ultimately a choice. Even if peace is far away, we can decide to focus more on God's work than our own feelings. We can choose to live out the prayer of St. Francis of Assisi: "...Lord, may I not so much seek to be consoled as to console; to be understood as to understand; to be loved as to love. Because it is in giving that we receive, in pardoning that we are pardoned..." (Teresa, 1996, p. 8).

Thus we can choose to love even when we do not feel particularly hopeful, joyful, or happy. The work of love and salvation is about more than our feelings. There will be days when we feel heartbroken, discouraged, hurt, and angry. It would be unnatural and unhealthy if we never felt these important human emotions. We need them. They can be important clues that we need to take better care of ourselves, change our strategies, adjust relationships, or find roles in life better suited to our skills. But sometimes feelings are just feelings and we need to keep pushing through. If we let God in, miracles can happen in moments of heartbreak and grief. Whenever you find yourself despairing, turn to God. Offer Him your heart and your suffering, and invite Him to raise you to new life.

Above all, God desires for us to live our lives in accordance with the law of love. It is written in Amos 5: 23-24, "Away with your noisy songs! I will not listen to the melodies of your harps. But if you would offer me holocausts, then let justice surge like water, and goodness like an unfailing stream." I believe that God wants us to sing, go to worship services, and engage in rituals that allow us to dwell in joy and truth. However, all of these wonderful experiences are meaningless if they do not yield fruit in acts of loving service to our neighbors. If the feelings of love and joy do not come easily, start with simple acts of love, and pray that your heart follows your hands.

We are called to be the Body of Christ alive in the world today. We must not abandon our work. Listen to the words of the famous prayer often attributed to St. Teresa of Avila: "Christ has no body now but yours, no hands, no feet on earth but yours. Yours are the eyes through which he looks with compassion on this world. Yours are the feet with which he walks to do good. Yours are the hands, with which He blesses all the world..." (Graham, 2014, p. 92). God entrusts us with the mission to serve, to forgive, to share suffering in solidarity with our neighbors, to reach out in compassion, and to strive for justice. God trusts us. We must not let Him down.

The wars rage on, the horrors continue, the realities of illness and sin and death still haunt our lives. But we must remember that Christ has already won the ultimate victory, and the Holy Spirit lives in us today. God will always give us the strength, courage, wisdom, and hope we need to keep going. Jesus says in Matthew 5: 4, "Blessed are they who mourn, for they will be comforted." There will be times when we feel overcome by the sorrow of the world and our own lives. In these moments we must turn to God. He will transform our suffering into a force for healing, compassion, and justice. He will comfort us, and one day, love alone will remain. Until then, we must persist in love. Remember the words of 1 Corinthians 13: 4-8: "Love is patient, love is kind. It is not jealous, love is not pompous, it is not inflated, it is not rude, it does not seek its own interests, it is not quick-tempered, it does not brood over injury, it does not rejoice over wrongdoing but rejoices with the truth. It bears all things, believes all things, hopes all things, endures all things. Love never fails…"

Love,

Aaron

PART THREE: LETTERS OF WISDOM: Let God be your guide through the twisting roads of relationships.

FOR THE EARLY DAYS OF DATING SOMEONE NEW

"I will show you what someone is like who comes to me, listens to my words, and acts on them. That one is like a person building a house, who dug deeply and laid the foundation on rock; when the flood came, the river burst against the house but could not shake it because it had been well built. But the one who listens but does not act is like a person who built a house on the ground without a foundation. When the river burst against it, it collapsed at once and was completely destroyed."

- Luke 6: 47-49

Dear Brother, Dear Sister, Dear Friend,

I wonder how dating has been for you so far. Is it fun and exciting? Is it terrifying? Have most of your dates thus far been boring and unremarkable? Awkward and embarrassing? Thrilling? Disappointing? All of the above? Many of us start dating, or start dating someone new, without knowing what to expect. The social rules and expectations of dating can seem confusing, intimidating, or unclear, especially for people in the gay world. There are so many mixed messages and it can be hard to navigate the waters. Confusion or feeling out of step with the crowd can lead to a sense of insecurity, and this makes dating a lot less fun than it could be.

In this letter, I hope to share with you some wisdom I have gained through dating experiences over the years. I do not claim to be an expert, but I have learned some hard lessons along the way, and I would love to help spare you some heartache.

The early days of dating are all about getting to know someone. If things go well, the first few weeks can help build the foundation of a new relationship, whether it be romantic or friendly. It takes time, faithfulness, selfless love, and honesty to build a strong foundation. As Jesus says in Luke 6: 47-49, "I will show you what someone is like who comes to me, listens to my words, and acts on them. That one is like a person building a house, who dug deeply and laid the foundation on rock; when the flood came, the river burst against the house but could not shake it because it had been well built. But the one who listens but does not act is like a person who built a house on the ground without a foundation. When the river burst against it, it collapsed at once and was completely destroyed." Relationships are like houses. They need sturdy foundations built carefully over long periods of time if they are going to last.

When dating, it is helpful to know ahead of time the kind of person you are looking for. When you are single, dream about the qualities you hope to find in your soul mate. Think about the things you would like to do with them and for them. Imagine who might be the right fit for you. Write these things down in a journal. Make lists. And then pray over all your thoughts and ideas. When you start dating someone new, ask God how they compare to the person you have always dreamed about. Open your heart to God and ask the Holy Spirit to speak to your heart. Be open to the possibility that God may have someone in mind for you who challenges you and loves you better than you dreamed possible. Ask God to help you discern which qualities are non-negotiable deal-breakers, and which are things you would like but could do without. Ask what God thinks about this new person in your life.

Many will tell you to avoid deep subjects on the first few dates, as this might scare people away or rush things along too quickly. I say it helps to just let conversation flow naturally and to not worry about it too much. If you get nervous before or during dates, plan activities where you can move and shake out some nerves along the way. For example, you can take a walk together or play a game of basketball. Alternatively, you could play a board game to keep yourself mentally distracted or cook together so there is a task to focus on. Make sure to plan something fun after the date ahead of time, such as hanging out with a friend or reading on your couch with a chocolate sundae. Even if the main event is a humiliating disaster, you can remind yourself that it will all be over soon enough and you have good things to look forward to later in the day.

Dating can be bizarre sometimes. As Christians, we are called to build our lives around love, to give ourselves in love for one another, to live with integrity and honesty. We are called to loving relationships. As Jesus says in John 13: 35, "This is how all will know that you are my disciples, if you have love for one another." In established relationships, the ways I am meant to love becomes clear, at least some of the time. I might be called to love my grandmother by visiting her in the hospital when she is sick and taking her out to lunch when she is well. I might be called to love my sister by consoling her when her heart is broken and laughing with her when we rant about our stressful days at work. Those of us who are parents are called to care for every need of our children, nurture their growth, and teach them how to live. Those of us who are spouses or in long-term committed relationships are called to be loving and faithful partners, bear each other's burdens, and hold one another in the good times and the bad.

We are called to love our neighbors as ourselves, and we are even commanded to love our enemies. In short, we are called to love everyone. But what is the proper way to love someone in the early days of dating? When I do not know this person very well, but I want to know them better, how can I love them? How should I show love for them?

Should I give myself completely to this person and be ever available to serve their needs from day one? Should I maintain a selfish attitude and be constantly evaluating whether this person fits into my life and serves my needs? There is a balance between these extremes. Dating practices vary greatly among cultures, and we all have our unique expectations, histories, losses, hopes, dreams, and ideals that we bring to the dating table. To make sense of all this, we need to prayerfully reflect on what dating is and what it means to date somebody. In my opinion, God has made it clear that marriage is a loving and lifelong commitment between two people who want to make a family together, but the way people get there varies a lot. Therefore, dating can be whatever we make it to be. At its best, dating can be a way for two people to get to know each other, enjoy spending time together, and build a sense of how they would like to relate to each other moving forward— as friends, as people in love, as spouses, or not at all.

But dating can be more than an interview process for a life partner. It can be fun in and of itself. If a date is awkward, then laugh about it on the inside and memorize every excruciating detail so you can tell a friend about it later. If spending time with someone makes your heart race and your face light up, then enjoy it for however long it lasts. If relationships do not work out, it does not make anyone a failure. Each attempt at dating is an opportunity to learn something about ourselves, about the kind of person we want to be with, and about how relationships work. At the end of the day, if the other person likes you and you do not really like them, tell them you would like to be friends and trust that they will move on to someone who truly wants to be with them. If you like them but they do not like you, let them go and trust that your person will come along eventually. And if you both like each other, keep enjoying each other and let the relationship build into whatever it is meant to be.

When dating, I think it is best to move slowly, both emotionally and physically. In the early days, take time to talk and take time to listen. Discuss your likes and dislikes. Share about your passions, what you do with your time, and what brings you joy. Do fun things together, like going for picnics or long walks or movie marathons. Try not to force anything emotionally. Let yourself like this other person a little, a lot, or not very much at all. Try not to run away if things feel intense in a good but scary way. Just spend time together, get to know each other, and let the relationship grow naturally into what it is meant to be. It might turn into burning love or friendship or a bland feeling that there is not much of a connection at all. Only time will tell. We must be patient. As it says in Proverbs 16: 32, "A patient man is better than a warrior, and he who rules his temper, than he who takes a city."

It can be tempting to rush things physically and emotionally. The desire for connection and touch often becomes intense and painful if we are long deprived of sweet compliments, tender words, hand holding, kissing, cuddling, sex, and all those many manifestations of affection and intimacy. As gay Christians, we may have spent time denying ourselves even hope for romantic love, and this makes the longing even more powerful. In addition to all this, we live in a culture that often encourages instant sex without emotional bonds or commitment. We are taught that hooking up for make-out sessions or one-night-stands is normal and even healthy. Many argue that to refrain from this behavior by choice is an act of repression. This is a tricky subject area, because I do believe that as gay people, we are taught by society to be ashamed of our sexualities. We must resist such hurtful and oppressive messages. However, in my experience, sex without emotional intimacy and commitment leads to feelings of sadness and emptiness. One-night-stands and relationships built only on sexual gratification often result in people getting seriously hurt.

When we use others for sex without deep meaning, we fail to respect the full human dignity of the other people and ourselves. Our souls and our bodies are not separate pieces that cohabitate the same space. We cannot disconnect our libidos from our hearts, and we cannot turn our emotions on and off with a switch. Rather, our flesh and our spirits unite to make us human beings created in the image of God. To be healthy and whole, a connection of the body must always go along with a connection of the heart and soul. Otherwise, we lie with our bodies and tear ourselves up inside. Furthermore, as Christians, we realize that we carry the Holy Spirit of God in us. Everything we say and do must witness to the truth of who God is. As is written in Romans 8: 10, "But if Christ is in you, although the body is dead because of sin, the spirit is alive because of righteousness." As we get to know someone new and as our relationships grow, we must remember that we testify to who God is by how we live our lives and how we treat the people around us.

If we rush into bed with someone in the early stages of dating, it can be really hard to sort out our true feelings. We might wake up and ask ourselves, do I love him or do I just like having sex with him? Does she love me or is she using me to keep her warm at night? If we go from one random encounter to another, we are treating our partners as objects that provide a moment of pleasure, satisfaction, distraction, or relief from loneliness. Is this the way we want to be treated? Is this what we were made for? Is sex meant to be more than this? And even if we feel fine drifting from one lover to the next, how many people do we leave pining for us when we decide it is time to leave? How many people do we hurt? How many people have given up on true love in part because of the hurt we caused by using them and walking away?

If we want to build a lasting bond with someone, if we want to find true love, or if we want to minimize how much we hurt others, it is wise to take things slow. I am not saying to build up walls of ice in the early days of dating. Allow yourself to enjoy the journey! Sometimes we fall really hard really fast, and that can be exciting, wonderful, and good in many ways! An early rush of attraction can be intense, but it usually takes time for feelings to grow deep. A wise counselor once told me that there is a difference between intensity and depth, and depth alone is lasting. It is wise to make sure our physical expression of affection progresses at the same pace as emotional depth in our relationships. Sexuality and attachment are sacred. We must approach matters of the heart with thoughtfulness and responsibility. Allow God to guide you. As it says in Lamentations 3: 25, "Good is the Lord to one who waits for him, to the soul that seeks him."

Overall, the best advice I can give is to be honest with yourself and the person you date about who you are, what you believe, what you value, what you feel, and what you want. People get hurt when we are too afraid or self-doubting to be honest from the beginning. When I started dating in my mid-twenties, I had repressed the romantic side of myself for so long that I had grown desperate to form an intimate bond with somebody. As soon as I started dating someone new, I would convince myself I had deep feelings for this person, even if I did not. The truth is that I was tired of being alone. If I could tell someone liked me, I tried my best to like them because I wanted to be with somebody and I hated the thought of hurting their feelings. I did not yet realize how painfully dishonest this was. And so I fell into a pattern of lying to myself and the people I was dating about how I was feeling, which always resulted in people getting hurt. I wish I had the courage to be more honest from the beginning.

The truth is that we will all probably make mistakes in the realm of dating and love. Sometimes we become so desperate for a sense of belonging or intimacy that we do things we know are wrong. Sometimes we fall into habits that feel good even though we know they hurt other people or ourselves. Sometimes we get confused, we lose sight of what is right, and we act irresponsibly without thinking about the consequences. When this happens, it is important to remember that God's mercy is at the heart of our Christian faith. We are saved and redeemed by God. Whenever we fall, God is waiting to lift us up, forgive us, grace us with deeper wisdom, and grant us the strength to live more faithfully to the law of love.

Scripture is full of messages promising God's healing and forgiveness. Psalm 103: 12 says, "As far as the east is from the west, so far have our sins been removed from us." Micah 7: 18-19 asks, "Who is there like you, the

God who removes guilt and pardons sin for the remnant of his inheritance; who does not persist in anger forever, but delights rather in clemency, and will again have compassion on us, treading underfoot our guilt? You will cast into the depths of the sea all our sins." Again we read in Acts 3: 19, "Repent, therefore, and be converted, that your sins may be wiped away." We are saved in Christ, who suffered greatly and died that he might rise again and bring us with him to new life. Learn from your mistakes and failures, but do not let them keep you from experiencing the love of God. God cannot live and love through you if you are obsessed with your own imperfections. None of us are perfect, but God is perfect, and if we trust in Him, He will help us grow into the people we were made to be.

Dating is a personal journey that we each need to figure out with God's help. As you begin any new dating adventure, I invite you to pray. Ask God to guide you as you get to know this person. Ask God to show you how you are called to love each other and where the relationship should go next. Listen, and be open to any answer.

If you find yourself single time and time again, take time to connect with friends and good people in your life. I have learned over time that there is a big difference between being alone and being single. There is always someone nearby for you to love, and the love of friends, family, and God are just as rapturous as romantic love. Try not to take dating too seriously, protect yourself, and when the right person comes along, any walls you have built up will come crashing down, one by one.

At the end of the day, try not to worry too much about dating or even relationships. Like everything else in life, romantic love has its ups and downs. We need to remember that the anchor of our hope is always Christ. If we keep him at the center and remember we are called to love everyone we encounter each day, dating loses its stress and becomes a fun adventure. As it says in Romans 15: 13, "May the God of hope fill you with all joy and peace in believing, so that you may abound in hope by the power of the holy Spirit." Relationships are placed in their proper perspective when we see them as one of many avenues through which we can share the love God gives us with others. As Jesus says in Matthew 6: 33, "But seek first the kingdom of God and his righteousness, and all these things will be given you besides."

If you are single, love and serve God in your singleness. If you are dating someone new, love and serve God in how you approach this new adventure in your life. And when the light of true love grows in your heart, love and serve God by loving your soul mate. Whatever stage you find yourself in, embrace the mission of seeking God and inviting Him into your heart so that He can live more deeply in the world through you.

Love,

Aaron

FOR WHEN YOU WONDER IF YOU ARE READY FOR SEX

"For I am convinced that neither death, nor life, nor angels, nor principalities, nor present things, nor future things, nor powers, nor height, nor depth, nor any other creature will be able to separate us from the love of God in Christ Jesus our Lord."

- Romans 8: 38-39

Dear Sister, Dear Brother, Dear Friend,

It seems like you have some very exciting things to think about these days! Maybe you have someone special in your life and you are discerning whether or not you want to be with them in an intimate way. Or maybe you are thinking about whether or not you should go on the hunt for someone to hook up with. Maybe you feel your sexuality coming more and more to life, and you want to share your body, your energy, your beautiful self with another person.

First, let me say how wonderful and good it is to ponder these things and to live as a sexual being. We are often taught to be ashamed of our nakedness, our desires, our thirst to connect in passion with someone we want who wants us, too. These longings are sacred and holy. We do not have to be afraid or ashamed of them. Rather, we need to acknowledge they are gifted to us by a loving and creative God. We need to listen and let God guide us as we live out our sexual lives, just like we should let God guide us in everything else. Is now the right time for sex? Is this the right person? Is sexual intimacy the right way to love this person, and is it the right way to love them today? The truth is that sex is powerful and must be treated with compassionate responsibility. Sexual union can lead to deep love and joy, or it can leave people deeply hurt and broken inside.

Notice that this is not a letter only about having sex for the first time. We always must be intentional and purposeful with how we live out our sexualities. Some Christian groups focus a lot on when one should give up one's virginity, and this single-mindedness often leaves people wondering what to do if they have already had sex. Putting too much focus on virgin or not-virgin status can make people feel like they have to choose between two extremes and, if they have ever had sex, they are led to believe they may as well give up trying to be thoughtful because it is too late for them. This mentality is painfully warped. Sexual morality should not be a legalistic set of rules that get thrown out the window after one crosses a certain threshold. Thinking and praying about being ready for sex, regardless of one's past, is a lifelong commitment to love one's self and others.

So is it right? Is now the time? Is this the person you should be with? How can anybody know for sure?

First, pray about all the questions you have and all the decisions you have to make. Ask God to open your eyes and move your heart to do what is right. Listen to what the Holy Spirit speaks to your heart. Are you wanting to have sex now because you think you are supposed to, or because you truly want to from the depths of your soul? Do you trust the person you want to be with? Will they love you and cherish you, or do they seem ready to bail once they get what they want? How well do you know this person? Is it important to you that you share sex only with someone you really love? What is the purpose of sex, and are you both ready to live out that purpose with each other?

Once again, I encourage you to explore these questions in prayer with God. I am convinced that love and commitment are essential pieces of joyful, healthy, and fulfilling sexual relationships. Traditional Christian beliefs hold that sexuality has two purposes. The first is to unite two people in a bond of love, and the second is to bring new life into the world. I sincerely believe that two people of the same gender can accomplish both these purposes through sex. Two people of the same gender who love each other can certainly find delight and connection through sexual union. And though two bodies of the same sex cannot literally create a baby without the miraculous intervention of God, sex shared between a same-gendered couple can bring new life to the world spiritually through the joy and energy they create through their union. The energy and love born from any loving couple flows outward through their lives into the world.

Looking around, I see a lot of people choosing to have sex without love. To me, this feels empty and sad. Sometimes people are so desperate for a sense of intimacy or connection that they have sex with strangers or near-strangers. They are simply trying to fill a void. Brief sexual encounters might feel good for a little while, but the painful emptiness always comes back because it was never filled with anything true or lasting. Our need for intimacy cannot be filled by sex without love. Our hearts and bodies naturally yearn for commitment, kindness, respect, and connection with someone both physically and emotionally.

Some people rush into sex out of fear. Perhaps they are afraid of being unlovable, of losing out on what life has to offer, of being an inexperienced freak or loser. Or perhaps they are afraid deep down that there is something wrong with them for being gay and they try to chase this feeling away by rushing into sex as an act of rebellion. If this applies to you in any way, remember that the antidotes to fear are always faith and love. We do not need to be afraid because we can place our trust in the God who made us and loves us unconditionally. As it says in 1 John 4: 18, "There is no fear in love, but perfect love drives out fear because fear has to do with punishment, and so one who fears is not yet perfect in love."

If you choose to have sex outside of love because you are desperate, curious, afraid, or simply overcome with desire, please know that this will never stop God from loving you. As is written in Romans 8: 38-39, "For I am convinced that neither death, nor life, nor angels, nor principalities, nor present things, nor future things, nor powers, nor height, nor depth, nor any other creature will be able to separate us from the love of God in Christ Jesus our Lord." God loves you, holds you, and wants you with a passionate blaze of unquenchable fire. Do not let anyone tell you that God has stopped loving you. If you sin, remember that God forgives us when we turn to Her, and what you did in the past is less important than what you choose to do in the future. Jesus says in Luke 5: 32, "I have not come to call the righteous to repentance but sinners." The truth is, we are all sinners. We all need God.

I am not worried about whether or not you follow a set of rules about sex. Rather, I am hopeful that you respect yourself and any person you choose to be intimate with. I want you to see yourself and others as human beings created, known, and loved by God. I hope and pray that you are careful and tender with your body and with their body, with your heart and with their heart. I hope and pray that any way you choose to live out your sexuality has at its core a true desire to bring joy, love, beauty, and life into the world. I hope you truly seek the will of God, who is love, in all your choices. As is written in 1 Corinthians 6:19, "Do you not know that your body is a temple of the holy Spirit within you, whom you have from God, and that you are not your own?" At the end of the day, we are a part of the Body of Christ, and we are called to give everything to God.

Follow your conscience with sex, as in all things. Listen to where God is calling you and discern what you believe is right. The world will try to break down your beliefs and tell you what to think. Some will tell you never to have sex, that gay sex is always wrong. Some will tell you to have sex whenever you want without caring about emotional connection, commitment, or consent. It can feel so lonely to seek sexual virtue as a gay Christian.

Furthermore, some of us approach sex with deep fear and anxiety even in the context of loving and committed relationships. Sometimes we are so hurt by internalized shame, self-hatred, or low self-esteem that we are terrified by the idea of being completely naked and open with anyone, even our soul mates. In particular, survivors of sexual abuse or assault often find it difficult to experience joy, peace, or emotional intimacy through sex. No matter what has happened to you in the past, I want you to know that your body and your sexuality belong to you alone. There is no commandment that you need to have sex. You get to choose when and with whom you would like to be intimate.

If someone ignored your human dignity and forced, coerced, or tricked you into some kind of sexual contact, please know that you are not broken. You are not dirty. You are not ugly. You are a beautiful, powerful, and beloved child of God. I wish I could ease your pain and even erase it with my words, but I can't do that. I can't take your journey away from you.

But I promise that you are not alone. God is with you every step of the way. And though it may not seem like it, there are legions of survivors and allies who stand beside you on the path to healing and resurrection. If you let Her, God will guide you to the support you need. Psalm 147: 2-4 says, "The LORD rebuilds Jerusalem, gathers the dispersed of Israel, heals the brokenhearted, binds up their wounds, numbers all the stars, calls each of them by name." In time, you will feel safe and at home again in your own body. Many people find profound healing as they work with counselors and trusted loved ones to build coping skills, make meaning of past experiences, and discover hope for the future. In addition, some communities offer support groups where survivors of sexual abuse and assault come together to tell their stories and lift each other up. To connect with professional support, please call the National Sexual Assault Telephone Hotline at 1-800-656-4673, the

National Suicide Prevention Lifeline at 1-800-273-8255, or the Trevor Project at 1-866-488-7386.

If you struggle with fear and anxiety when it comes to sex for any reason, you are not alone. Try to let go of the pressure to be anything other than who you are and who God calls you to be today. Refuse to let anyone make you feel inferior or worthless. Seek out relationships with friends, teachers, ministers, and mentors who want what is good for you. You deserve to be surrounded by people who love you for who you are. It may not seem like it now, but through a unique story that only you and God can write together, you will find healing. If you want to enjoy sex, you will someday, when the time is right.

For years, I thought that being gay meant I had to be celibate forever. This led to a profound sense of loneliness and despair. After years of Scripture study, prayer, and conversations with spiritual leaders and other people in my life, I came to believe that love was always a gift from God, for God was love. I stretched my thinking around what it means to "create new life" and realized that gay couples bring new life into the world through the joy and energy born of their union. Some couples even make families through adoption. In time, I grew open to the possibility of falling in love and, when the time was right, having sex.

Once I opened myself to the possibility of dating, I thought that I had endured the most difficult part of the journey. I had overcome oppressive ideas embedded in religion through ignorance and human shortcomings. I thought I was free at last. I quickly realized that there was a new journey to embark upon, and that was learning how to maintain my beliefs and live out my values in communities of gay people, many of whom spurned and rejected my beliefs. My heart breaks often to this day. I believe many people in the gay community reject faith and mainstream sexual ethics, such as monogamy, because they have been deeply hurt and disillusioned by their own experiences with religious communities. I wish I could say I always approach differences of opinion with openness, mercy, and grace, but sometimes it just hurts.

Shortly after coming out, I told a gay Christian spiritual director that I wanted to wait until I was married to have sex. He told me, "If you do that, I don't think anyone will ever want you." His words left me devastated and broken. It felt like a confirmation of my greatest fear, that I was unlovable, that my beliefs were unrealistic, that if I wanted to be with someone, I had to fundamentally change myself and how I approached relationships.

I never want you to feel that way. Through prayer and deep reflection, I want you to develop your own beliefs with the grace and leadership of God. I want you to know joy in the search for God's truth, not fear or an overwhelming sense that you must always rationalize and defend what you believe. Feelings of loneliness are a part of life, but I want you to know that wherever you stand, you are never alone. God loves you. I love you. Think and pray. Do not stop searching until you come to a sense of peace and joy in your decisions about sex. Love as God made you to love, and be happy.

Through deep soul-searching, observation, study, and experience, I have come to believe that there is deep beauty and goodness in sexuality within a loving, committed, monogamous relationship. When two people remain faithful to one another and allow sex to be a special language shared between them, this creates a special bond of intimacy and trust that is fundamental to the formation of a happy, healthy, loving relationship. At the end of the day, it is so romantic to think about sharing sex with that one special person.

There have been times in my life when I gave up on the idea of ever finding true love, and yet I still felt an intense craving for connection and intimacy. In such moments of despair and doubt, I was deeply tempted to give up my ideals and do whatever it took to satisfy my own longings. All of a sudden it became easy to treat people like objects rather than as Temples of the Holy Spirit. The thing I learn over and over again is that sin hurts. When we do something wrong or fail to do something good, we disconnect ourselves from God, from others, and from the best version of ourselves. God never stops loving us no matter what, but when we sin, we turn our backs on God.

Her love remains, but we shut ourselves off from it, little by little or all at once. Sexual immorality is not about breaking moral codes or being a bad person. Rather, sexual sin happens when we hurt others or ourselves, when we use people, when we break promises, when we lie, when we see people as things that exist only to make us feel good rather than as human beings known and loved by God.

Of course, for your own protection and for your partner's health, it is important to educate yourself about sexually transmitted infections and safer sex practices. Know that some diseases are transmitted through body fluids and some are spread through skin to skin touch. Utilize whatever methods make sense for the choices you make. It only makes sense to consider not using protection when partners commit to only having sex with each other and test negative for all diseases at least six months after making this commitment. If this does not apply to you, then protect yourself and protect your partner every time.

Communication about sex, what it means, and whether or not we are ready for it is key to a happy and fulfilling sex life. This is true even for long-term committed couples. It is hurtful when one person in a couple believes they have found their soul mate and the other feels like they are just having a good time. It is sexual assault when sex happens without consent. Our culture teaches people in both subtle and overt ways to seek sex without asking first. Our culture also teaches subtly to ignore protests. We need to change all this, and we can start in our own relationships. As you embark on relationships and sex, know what your intentions are and make them clear to your partner. If you want sex, make sure the other person wants it, too. Talk about it. If you are not ready to talk about it, you are not ready for sex.

Overall, take your time in exploring your sexuality. There is no need to rush. Sex should be a joyful and exciting journey that feels good physically, emotionally, and spiritually. Sex is nothing to be ashamed of. If you make choices that hurt yourself or others, then apologize to God and any person you harmed, do what you can to make peace, and forgive yourself. Try not to obsess over sexual sins. If you do something wrong, repent and move on. Your emotional energy is needed for acts of love and justice in the world, not ongoing self-punishment. Sex and relationships can often be difficult, messy, confusing, and complicated. Pray, and talk to trusted loved ones. Ask for help with sorting through all the questions and decisions you have to make. Do not put pressure on yourself to do anything more than what you are ready for today. It is okay to start with kisses on cheeks and holding hands. It is okay to dream about passionate love-making. Listen to your heart, think, pray, and trust that God will guide you if you let Her.

Love,

Aaron

FOR THE DAY YOUR HEART IS BROKEN

"I will give you a new heart and place a new spirit within you, taking from your bodies your stony hearts and giving you natural hearts. I will put my spirit within you and make you live by my statutes, careful to observe my decrees."

\- Ezekiel 36: 26-27

Dear Brother, Dear Sister, Dear Friend,

Love between human beings is an amazing gift, but it comes with the risk of one day ending. If love is true, it never really ends, but it does change. There is a deep and ugly pain that comes with heartbreak. Opening ourselves up to another person takes incredible courage. Sometimes relationships take us on ecstatic flights of joy and we think we'll never come down to earth ever again. And then suddenly she leaves you, or he betrays you, or they hurt you, or the feelings that once felt like the sun in your chest fade into nothing. You find yourself crashing to the ground, devastated and alone, and you wonder how you got there.

A heart can be broken in so many ways. Sometimes we walk into a room and find our one true love entangled with someone else. Sometimes the person we thought we would be with forever tells us they do not love us anymore, or that they never loved us at all. Sometimes we want someone to be ours but they never seem to see us. This person might be a hopeless crush, but it also might be a parent, a sibling, or an old friend who left us behind. Sometimes somebody we care about hurts us, physically or emotionally. Sometimes we lose someone we love dearly to death. Grief makes us hate the world for continuing to spin without them. Sometimes our hearts are broken not by people but by some devastating defeat in life. We do not get into the school of our dreams, or we give up going to college because we need to work to support the family, or we fail to get the job or the promotion we thought we deserved, or the part in the play, or the spot in the band. For a while, we feel like we never want to love or dream again.

And sometimes there is never a climactic tragedy at all, but our hearts shatter into pieces, little by little, every day. As I was growing up, the thing I wanted most in the world was to fall in love, get married, and make a family of my own. Over time, bit by bit, voices in the world and in my own head picked away at this dream. They told me love does not last, or that two men could never be faithful to each other, or that I was not good enough or handsome enough or cool enough or confident enough to be a man that somebody could want. Soon enough my heart was nothing but an embittered mess of broken dreams.

It breaks my heart anew to know that you are reading this letter and nursing your own wounds. I am so sorry for your loss, your hurt, your pain. Whatever happened, you do not deserve this suffering. This is a part of your journey that must be endured and can only be overcome with God's grace. I wish I could make it easier.

Please remember that you need not go through this alone. When you are ready, talk to trusted people about your heartache and let them support you. As always, cling to God, for He is with you. God will hold you in your sorrow and put you back together again, piece by piece. In time, your healing will be a symbol of the ultimate salvation God promises to all of us. As it says in Revelation 21: 4, "He will wipe every tear from their eyes, and there shall be no more death or mourning, wailing or pain, for the old order has passed away."

One of the tragic truths of the human condition is that people do not love perfectly, at least not this side of heaven. We fall short of the selfless, generous, faithful, and honest ideals modeled for us by Jesus. We are broken by sin and our moral vision is clouded by insecurities, fears, prejudices, lusts, and pride. When your heart is broken, you face not only your own personal tragedy, but also the evidence and weight of all the sin in all the world. This pain exists because we are not perfect. We hurt each other because we are flawed.

And yet, that is not all we are. We are loved by God, and God offers redemption to all. In times of suffering, it can feel like we are abandoned by God, but nothing could be farther from the truth. In fact, God is with us intimately in our hurt. He suffers beside us. If we offer our pain to Jesus, we join him on the cross and our suffering unites with his for the redemption of our world. As Christians, we believe that the Hebrew Scriptures testify to the coming of our Lord, Jesus. Listen to the words of Isaiah 53: 4-5: "Yet it was our infirmities that he bore, our sufferings that he endured, while we thought of him as stricken, as one smitten by God and afflicted. But he was pierced for our offenses, crushed for our sins, upon him was the chastisement that makes us whole, by his stripes we were healed." Jesus suffered for us that we might be saved. When we suffer with broken hearts, we can offer that pain to God and spend our time on the cross with Jesus that we might die with him and, in time, be raised with him to new life.

If we open ourselves to God, He will teach us how to love more truly, fully, and deeply. He will heal our brokenness and show us what love really is. This is why we must pray for those who hurt us. When our hearts are broken, it is easy to succumb to violence in our thoughts, words, or deeds. It feels natural to hate or judge those who hurt us, to hate or judge ourselves for somehow not being good enough and bringing on this pain.

It can be healthy to let your feelings be as they will be in the middle of an emotional crisis. You need to take time to grieve, to be sad, angry, or confused. Feel the feelings and let them move you to think, grow, create, talk, and do what you need to do as you make meaning of the storm inside you. But throughout the journey, offer your thoughts, feelings, and actions to God. Let Him move you to where He wants you to be. Whoever hurt you probably did so because they were hurt by someone else before they met you. So now you have a choice. Will you let the pain of injury or grief flow through you to add even more hate and violence to the world? Or will you open your broken heart to God so that He may fill you with healing grace and transform your misery into mercy, understanding, and, with time, peace?

Meditate on the questions you need to ask and seek the answers in God. Why did he betray you? Why did she lie to you? Why does your dad never talk to you anymore? Why did your mom walk out? What happened to them? Where is your loved one now? Are they happy? How does God see the person who hurt or abandoned you? What path do you need to take today? How can you set your spirit free from the pain of this experience?

If you allow God to heal you in this moment, you will stop the cycle of sin and pain. As Jesus is crucified, we read in John 19: 25, "Standing by the cross of Jesus were his mother and his mother's sister, Mary the wife of Clopas, and Mary of Magdala." Take some time to picture this image. Mary and these other faithful disciples *stand* at the foot of the cross as Jesus undergoes great agony and death. Mary faced the greatest of torments when she watched her son tortured and killed, yet she stood by him in love, and she did this in solidarity with other loved ones who never left her side. She teaches us by example how to grieve while also following the way of her son and our God, Jesus.

Stopping the cycle of sin is especially important for the gay community. So many of us have been hurt in so many ways. Pain has come to us through families, friends, teachers, media messages, churches, lovers, and our own internalized hate. Sometimes we hide our suffering or pretend it is not there, but at some point it often explodes in our relationships. We need to heal our broken hearts to stop ourselves from breaking the hearts of others.

So how does one go about healing a broken heart? Pray and ask God to help you. Seek God in the quiet, in nature, in Scripture, in music, and in art. Let God find you in conversations with trusted family, mentors, and friends. Express your pain and your growth through poetry, painting, dance, writing, sports, or whatever creative outlet works for you. Engage in activities that are life-giving. At the end of the day, give it all to God and let Him work in you. As it says in Exodus 14: 14, "The LORD himself will fight for you; you have only to keep still."

Resist the temptation to isolate yourself. Hiding away from life will give you plenty of time to lick your wounds, but the only salve that can truly heal you is the love of God and other people. We cannot fix ourselves, and spending too much time meditating on our own pain will move us deeper into bitterness. If we open ourselves in vulnerability to people we trust, it lets them know that they can share their burdens with us as well. If we are brave and reach out to others, we learn that we are not the only ones in the world with broken hearts. And we learn that we can help those who help us.

It can be tempting to run away from pain in drugs, alcohol, empty sex, or some other self-destructive vice. These things might feel good for a moment, or they might numb everything for a while. But the pain always returns when the high is over and brings with it a new mess of hurt. Each human being is a Temple of the Holy Spirit. God dwells in you and the people around you. Our human dignity demands that we treat ourselves and each other with love and respect, even when we hurt. It is hard to do this when our minds and hearts are clouded by substances, when we treat other people like objects, when we place ourselves and our pain at the center of the universe and use it to rationalize things we know are wrong.

I had a yoga teacher who lost her sister to suicide. Torn with grief, one of her mentors told her, "Sit with the pain and it will awaken you." These words changed her life, and this story changed mine. If we deaden ourselves to pain with drugs, sex, denial, or sin of any kind, we avoid the hurt but we also fail to grow. We push the hurt behind a wall and fail to build foundations of understanding, compassion, or forgiveness.

Do not hide from the pain. Sit with it, let God sit with you, and allow yourself to be awakened. As it says in Ephesians 5: 14, "...for everything that becomes visible is light. Therefore, it says: 'Awake, O sleeper, and arise from the dead, and Christ will give you light.'"

People will break our hearts, but we serve a God who works miracles. Listen to the promises of Ezekiel 36: 26-27: "I will give you a new heart and place a new spirit within you, taking from your bodies your stony hearts and giving you natural hearts. I will put my spirit within you and make you live by my statutes, careful to observe my decrees." God is perfect love. He will never betray us and never leave us. We even hold onto hope that those lost to death will rise to new life in Him. As it says in John 3: 16, "For God so loved the world that he gave his only son, so that everyone who believes in him might not perish but might have eternal life."

God can be mysterious. Sometimes we feel lost. But even when attacked by our greatest doubts and fears, He is with us. God will heal our lives if we let Him. As it says in Psalm 23: 4, "Even when I walk through a dark valley, I fear no harm for you are at my side; your rod and staff give me courage."

I am so sorry that you are hurting. I hope you heal and grow through your time in this dark valley. I hope you find someone soon who looks unflinchingly into your eyes and sees your truest self. I hope you find someone who listens to you and opens up to you about their own struggles so that you can support one another. I hope you feel God's presence in this moment and find in Him a love strong enough to carry all that you are, including the scars of this heartbreak.

Love,

Aaron

FOR WHEN THE TIME COMES TO BREAK
SOMEONE'S HEART

"For we do not have a high priest who is unable to sympathize with our weaknesses, but one who has similarly been tested in every way, yet without sin. So let us confidently approach the throne of grace to receive mercy and to find grace for timely help."

- Hebrews 4: 15-16

Dear Sister, Dear Brother, Dear Friend,

This letter is as difficult for me to write as I assume it is for you to read. Maybe you find yourself in a relationship that you know is not right. Maybe things moved too fast. Maybe you were swept away at first and you have slowly realized that you and this other person are not really compatible. Perhaps some part of you knew this person was not your soul mate from the beginning but you held on for experience or to not be alone. Maybe you put pressure on yourself to be with this person, you wanted above all else to avoid the guilt of hurting them, but the burden of dishonesty has become too heavy to bear.

Dating, feelings, and relationships can be messy, confusing, and painful. Sometimes people come together, sometimes they stay together, and sometimes they fall apart. It hurts so much to be abandoned by someone we love, and it hurts to leave. If you are wrestling with a difficult decision about whether or not to continue a relationship, turn to God. She will guide you if you let Her. As is written in Hebrews 13: 20-21, "May the God of peace, who brought up from the dead the great shepherd of the sheep by the blood of the eternal covenant, Jesus our Lord, furnish you with all that is good, that you may do his will. May he carry out in you what is pleasing to him through Jesus Christ, to whom be glory forever and ever. Amen."

Times get hard in any relationship, but that does not necessarily mean it is time to end things. Sometimes we feel the impulse to run as things get more serious. Intimacy can be scary for some of us, but if it is shared with the right person, the vulnerability of closeness is something to cherish and protect. Ask God if She wants you to push through the anxiety and stay.

Or maybe you are facing a different crossroads in a relationship. Maybe the initial rush of falling in love is over, but you have yet to learn the enduring depth of mature love. You may no longer lose yourself in idealized daydreams of who you thought this other person was, but if God wills it, you may be able to tenderly care for this other person and cherish them for who they truly are. True love changes with time, but it never dies. Maybe the love you share with this person is changing, but still true.

Perhaps you are discovering that there was never true love shared between the two of you. If this is the case, listen for God's voice. She may tell you it is time to end this chapter of your lives, turn to Her for healing, and move on.

I have had several dating experiences where things went way too fast. I told myself I liked the other person, but after a few weeks, I realized I was just desperate to not be alone. I ended things, and the other person was left hurting. I thought I had broken this habit when I met a good, kind man who wanted nothing more than to make me happy. I liked him very, very much. We dated a long time, and I told him I loved him. I thought this was the truth, and maybe it was. But over time, a feeling of wrongness grew in my heart. I wanted him to be happy. I wanted to make him happy. But I felt myself growing more distant. There were little differences between us that I thought I could live with, but suddenly they seemed insurmountable. I prayed and prayed until I realized I just could not continue being with him. I was horrified at my faithlessness and the painful reality of the truth: I wanted to break up.

I yearned to avoid talking to him about this, but it was the truth and we both had to face it. In John 14: 6, we read, "Jesus said to him, 'I am the way and the truth and the life. No one comes to the Father except through me.'" We need to live in the truth if we are to be followers of Christ. Relationships should never be exclusively about how I feel or what I want. Nor should they be exclusively about what the other person feels and wants. Feelings come and go, wax and wane. Relationships have their ups and downs. Searching for a soul mate is about more than finding the person who sets off your brain chemistry just right, and it is about more than finding someone who matches a predetermined checklist of qualities. We need to hand our romantic lives, along with the rest of ourselves, over to God. We need to ask God the hard questions and listen to the answers. God, is this the person you want me to be with? How do you want me to love this person, as a friend, as a person to date for now, as the love of my life? Do we help each other grow in love for you? Do we help each other grow into the people you created us to be? Can we be true partners to each other and work together for the important mission you have entrusted to us? Is there hope that we can remain together and become family to each other?

Ask these questions in prayer and listen to God. She will answer you. Trust Her. If in time you discern that God is not calling you to be with this person, then let them go. It may break their heart and yours, but heartbreak is better than living a lie. Loving a person involves seeking what is good for them, not doing everything you can to avoid hurting their feelings. There is always goodness in the truth, even if it hurts. If you end the relationship, you will both be free to search for love that will truly satisfy your souls and bring you both closer to God.

I sometimes think about the men I have hurt in the past. I worry they might still be hurting and alone. I pray for them. I thank them in my heart for all they taught me. I apologize for the ways in which I used them. I wish them peace, love, joy, and faith in the tender God who holds us all in Her warm embrace. I try to trust that God will care for them, heal any damage I caused, love them, and lead them to where they need to be.

Why do relationships that once seemed precious burn out, explode, turn cold, and fade away? Why do some relationships grow into joyful and fulfilling unions that mirror God's faithful love for Her people, and some relationships fall apart? I do not know. It is a mystery. But perhaps part of the answer lies in the fact that people are complex. We all carry within ourselves infinite layers of beliefs, values, desires, fears, insecurities, and dreams. Finding a soul mate takes time, and building a solid relationship requires dedicated effort.

Along the way, it is easy to make mistakes. In the game of romance, we are often blinded by confusing and mixed emotions, miscommunication, different expectations, and conflicting points of view. It takes time to get to know somebody and to discover one's own feelings. Gay people have some additional unique challenges. There are far fewer same-sex couple role models to show us what an authentic, honest, committed, loving relationship looks like. A lot of gay people wrestle with areas of internalized shame or self-loathing, and these elements often explode in the context of dating relationships. Sometimes after a long period of singleness or several heartbreaks, we start to believe we will never find a true or abiding romantic love. Rather than turning to God to carry us through devastation and pain, we sometimes decide to settle for what the world tells us is normal. We seek casual encounters, loveless physical intimacy, or relationships we know deep down are not right for us. In the end, these choices lead to people getting hurt, which adds to our guilt and often spirals into more hurtful behavior.

When we are haunted by our sins and mistakes, we need to trust in the absolute mercy of our loving God. Psalm 86: 5 says, "Lord, you are kind and forgiving, most loving to all who call on you." Ephesians 2: 4-5 says, "But God, who is rich in mercy, because of the great love he had for us, even when we were dead in our transgressions, brought us to life with Christ (by grace you have been saved)." Titus 3: 4-6 reads, "But when the kindness and generous love of God our savior appeared, not because of any righteous deeds we had done but because of his mercy, he saved us through the bath of rebirth and renewal by the holy Spirit, whom he richly poured out on us through Jesus Christ our savior." The truth is that Jesus knows us, understands us, and is waiting to forgive us as soon as we turn to him. As it says in Hebrews 4: 15-16, "For we do not have a high priest who is unable to sympathize with our weaknesses, but one who has similarly been tested in every way, yet without sin. So let us confidently approach the throne of grace to receive mercy and to find grace for timely help."

For many of us, sins related to dating and sexuality are some of the most painful areas of regret in our lives. But once we repent, apologize, and make the changes we need to make, we also need to let go of shame. Jesus did not suffer and die on the cross for us to dwell in misery, guilt, and self-loathing. As Jesus says in John 10: 9-10, "I am the gate. Whoever enters through me will be saved, and will come in and go out and find pasture. A thief comes only to steal and slaughter and destroy; I came so that they might have life and have it more abundantly." Jesus showed us how to live, and he rose from the dead so that we could rise with him.

So please, today, die to sins of dishonesty and selfishness. Die to guilt and shame, and rise to new life in Jesus Christ our Lord. Listen to God and step into the truth. If it is time to break someone's heart, then break it. Tell them the truth. Tell them everything. Admit your mistakes and apologize. Let them go. Let God take care of them. Pray for them. If you need it, pray for forgiveness, experience God's mercy, and trust in God's healing grace. Take time to grieve the loss of what you thought this relationship was going to be, and then move forward with your life. There is much adventure, love, and good work to be done for the both of you.

Love,

Aaron

FOR WHEN YOU FALL IN LOVE

"Set me as a seal on your heart, as a seal on your arm; for stern as death is love, relentless as the nether world is devotion; its flames are like a burning fire."

- Song of Songs 8: 6

Dear Brother, Dear Sister, Dear Friend,

Sometimes falling in love is a time of absolute joy. It feels like we fit in our own skin for the first time, like suddenly everything makes sense and every victory was worth the struggle. For some people, the early stage of romantic love is a blissful rush that sets them soaring through the clouds. Others experience a warm, quiet sense of peace that simply feels like home. Sadly, there are also times when strong attraction ushers in confusion, bittersweet sorrow, or pure agony. Whether new feelings of love bring delight or pain, discovering intense depths of passion make one feel alive in a whole new way.

Many of us grow up learning fairy tales and romances about star-crossed souls struggling to be together until they find their way to happily ever after. Contrary to what the pessimists say, I believe there is much to learn from fairy tales and romances. Like in real life, the protagonists of our famous love stories often face great adversity and hardship before finding their way to triumph. The characters often deal with common relationship issues such as miscommunication, difficulty building trust, and overcoming significant differences. These stories give us hope that if we treat one another with compassion, kindness, and respect, true love can indeed conquer all.

But the truth is that real love is not ultimately a fairy tale, a romance story, or even a feeling. Love is found when we give of ourselves for the happiness, well-being, growth, and salvation of another. As Christians, we know that true love is found on the cross. Jesus completed the greatest act of love for all time when he died on the cross and rose again to reunite us with God. 1 John 3:16 says, "The way we came to know love was that he laid down his life for us; so we ought to lay down our lives for our brothers" and sisters and friends. Likewise, Romans 5: 8 says, "But God proves his love for us in that while we were still sinners Christ died for us."

If true love is found on the cross, what does it mean to fall in love? What does it mean to love another person? These questions are related to each other, but they are different. The feelings of tenderness, attraction, and desire that we associate with "falling in love" can be a special and holy part of a loving relationship. These emotional elements often move us to live and act in love, but the feelings of tenderness, attraction, and desire are not in and of themselves love. Love happens when we choose to think, speak, and act in a way that honors and shows care for the beloved. This is why we can choose to love at all times, even when we do not feel like it. 1 Corinthians 13: 4-8 captures the essence of real love with the words, "Love is patient, love is kind. It is not jealous, love is not pompous, it is not inflated, it is not rude, it does not seek its own interests, it is not quick-tempered, it does not brood over injury, it does not rejoice over wrongdoing but rejoices with the truth. It bears all things, believes all things, hopes all things, endures all things. Love never fails..."

Are you in the early stages of falling in love with someone? Does your heart race in their presence? Does your stomach flip when you think about them? Do you feel like you want to do anything you can for them and give them everything you have to give?

Sometimes love hits us like a star falling from the sky. We meet someone and after one conversation we cannot help but want to get to know them more and more. And sometimes love comes gently and grows slowly in our hearts. We have a friend or someone we have been casually dating for a while who becomes more and more dear with time.

Perhaps you are deeply blessed in this season of life and you have come to love someone who loves you back. Congratulations, my friend. This indeed is an occasion of great joy. Drink in this moment. Enjoy it. Thank God for the blessing of this person in your life. Pray and ask God to help you both grow deeper in love for one another. If no one else is celebrating this moment with you, or if people in your life are telling you it is wrong to love someone of the same gender, please know that I joyously bless this new relationship. I see it as sacred, beautiful, and good, just like I see you as sacred, beautiful, and good.

As you embark on a new journey of love with this other person, be good to each other. Remain close to God as individuals and as a couple. For love to grow, it takes a commitment from both people to be faithful to one another, serve one another, and treat each other with kindness and respect. With this strong foundation, love will grow and become unshakable. As it says in Song of Songs 8: 6, "Set me as a seal on your heart, as a seal on your arm; for stern as death is love, relentless as the nether world is devotion; its flames are like a burning fire."

Take steps to protect your love by thanking each other for acts of kindness, giving each other warm and sincere compliments, and talking openly about issues in the relationship and differences of opinion as they come up. Also, remember that it is not realistic or fair to expect that all of your emotional needs will be met by one person. Enjoy being with the person you love, but also maintain healthy relationships with friends and family. Above all, maintain a strong relationship with God. God is the source of all love, goodness, and life. To be good to another person, we need to be full of the spirit of our living God.

Love sometimes fades or falls apart because people take advantage of each other, use each other, cut themselves off from people outside the relationship, or fail to give what they can to keep the other person happy and fulfilled. Love demands that both parties make sacrifices for the good of the other. The heart of love is found in the words of Jesus in Luke 6: 31 when he says, "Do to others as you would have them do to you."

For a relationship to be healthy, you both need to know your values and expectations, communicate them to each other, and hold each other accountable when mistakes are made. When I first started dating, I felt as if I had to be completely selfless. I thought I should never speak my mind and never ask for what I wanted or needed. I thought crushing my inner self was the best way to fully love someone. Whenever I approached relationships this way, things fell apart very quickly. Dating was an anxiety-producing burden and there was little love in any of it. It took time to realize that when I acted this way, the person I was dating could not really see me or know me at all. I was hiding behind a false, pretend selflessness. I was wearing a mask to make myself look like a warped version of the perfect Christian. There was no truth in it, and therefore it was not right.

I talked this over with a priest because I was truly confused. I could not reconcile my values with dating. I asked, "Father, we are taught to be selfless, so how can I love someone while also telling them what I feel, what I need, and what I want? How can I live out selfless love if I spend so much time talking about me? How can I ask someone to love me back when I am supposed to follow the model of God, who loves us unconditionally, who loves us when we do good and when we do evil?" My priest opened my eyes when he said, "Aaron, it is true God loves us unconditionally, but God wants us to love Him, too."

God yearns for our love. He leaves us free to love Him or not, and He loves us no matter what. But at the same time, He goes to great lengths to teach us how to love and remind us that we are commanded to love. Throughout the Scriptures, God makes covenants with our patriarchs and matriarchs, promising to be our God if we will be His people. God gives the law to Moses and the people of Israel so that they can walk in His ways, become a light to the nations, and share the truth of who God is and how God wants us to live. God sends the prophets to call His people back into right relationship with Him after they go astray. These prophets inspire us to give up false gods like wealth and power and turn to God through works of charity and justice. God sends His son and becomes incarnate as man in Jesus Christ the Messiah. Jesus teaches us to forgive, serve, and build peace, then dies and rises again to save us from our sins. God sends His Holy Spirit to live within us and guide us so that we can build up the Kingdom of God for the salvation of the world. Over and

139

over and over again, God takes countless opportunities to remind us that we are created to love God, love people, and love ourselves. In various gospels, Jesus himself quotes the words of Deuteronomy 6: 4-5, "Hear, O Israel! The LORD is our God, the Lord alone! Therefore, you shall love the LORD, your God, with all your heart, and with all your soul, and with all your strength."

God teaches us how to love Him, so we must follow His example and teach the people in our lives how to love us. This takes great courage because to let someone know what you want comes with the risk of not getting it. When this happens over and over, we need to ask ourselves if the person before us is ready to be in a deep, loving relationship. If the answer is no, we need to let them go, for our sake and theirs.

Contrary to fairy tale promises of happily ever after, the journey of love is not always joyous or fun. We all bring anxieties, insecurities, and fears into relationships. Part of true love is bringing all our messiness to the table so that the beloved can help us heal, grow, and change for the better. This takes time and effort. It is often painful, but if a couple sticks together through the process, it will help them grow closer to each other and deeper in love. Do not be afraid to be honest, challenge each other, and push one another to be the people God created you to be. If you do this, love will transform you in a sacred way.

And as you grow in love for one another, let that love overflow to bless the entire world. We are not given romantic love exclusively for our own enjoyment. Rather, this great gift should move our hearts and give us strength to go out and serve our neighbors and our God. Let Jesus speak to you through the words of Matthew 25: 35-36: "For I was hungry and you gave me food, I was thirsty and you gave me drink, a stranger and you welcomed me, naked and you clothed me, ill and you cared for me, in prison and you visited me." This is our calling as Christians, and whether we are single, dating, or married, this is the path of a loving life. Any affection we share in our personal relationships should give us energy to share greater love with the entire world.

One of the difficult things about the human condition is that we can develop feelings of infatuation for someone that we are not meant to love in a romantic sense. Sometimes we develop strong feelings of desire to be with a straight classmate, our best friend's partner, or the ex who hurt us in the past. As minorities in the population, gay Christians may feel like there are fewer opportunities to find someone to love, and this pressure may push us to fall for the wrong person. When this happens, it is easy to dwell in misery, self-pity, or jealousy. It is easy to pine away for someone who cannot or does not want to be with us, and it becomes tempting to think about scheming to make this person ours. Sometimes we become embittered or guilt-ridden due to our attractions, and so we curse our sexualities in general rather than accepting them and letting them be.

For my first serious crush, I fell really hard for a man I worked with in a group home for kids with emotional and behavioral issues. I loved watching this colleague of mine work with the young people. He was always smiling and making people laugh. I wanted to be like him. I had this goofy grin on my face whenever I thought about him. When I realized he was straight, it was like someone ripped my heart out of my chest and crushed it underfoot. After months of listening to tragic ballads alone in my room, I realized this did not have to be the end of the world. For some reason, God had given me eyes to see a great many wonderful things about this person. Thinking about him brought me joy. If I obsessed with the fact that he would never be my boyfriend, I would forever make myself unhappy. But when I praised God for making such a beautiful human being and prayed for his happiness without expecting anything for myself, I felt a profound sense of peace. And so, if you find yourself infatuated with someone who cannot be yours, then thank God for creating that person, praise God for all the good things you see in them, and pray that they find love and meaning in their life. Ask God to help you love them as you are meant to love them, as a neighbor of good will, a friend, or, in time, as something more.

Whether we find ourselves in the throes of passionate love, in the early stages of dating someone new, in the agony of unrequited love, or single without anything interesting on the near horizon, we need to remember that we all need God. If we feel anxious, confused, or afraid, we need Him to give us peace. If we feel elated and overjoyed, we must turn to Him in praise and thanksgiving for all the good He has showered upon us. This will increase our joy all the more. We must trust that our lives and relationships are in God's hands, and this is the best place for them to be. Enjoy loving God, loving others, and loving yourself. At the end of the day, this is why we are alive.

Love,

Aaron

PART FOUR: LETTERS OF HOPE AND STRENGTH:
Remember that God walks beside you through all your
struggles and all your victories.

FOR THE DAY YOU HATE YOUR BODY

"Not as man sees does God see, because man sees the appearance but the LORD looks into the heart."

- 1 Samuel 16: 7 B

"Now you are Christ's body, and individually parts of it."

- 1 Corinthians 12: 27

Dear Brother, Dear Sister, Dear Friend,

The world is full of messages that tell us we are not good enough. We are taught that we need to lose weight, build muscle, get ride of acne, change our hair, or alter the shapes of our noses. Words and images from media, peers, family, and our own heads warp the way we see ourselves. We lose sight of the beauty God gives us and the thrilling miracle that it is to be alive. We become paralyzed with hate for the shape of our bodies, the bumps and colors of our skin, the positioning of our eyes and noses, the measurements of our waists, or the curves underneath our shirts and pants. Sometimes there is little room left to love ourselves or others because our hearts and minds are crushed by overwhelming and exhausting self-loathing.

Negative self-esteem related to how we look often has devastating emotional consequences. When we hate our bodies and our faces, we often feel as if no one will ever

147

want us. Sometimes we feel ugly and unlovable, and to protect ourselves from rejection, we close our hearts to others and the world. We live like hermits. We might maintain casual relationships on the outside, but we always run away from true intimacy and hide the depths of what we feel, think, want, and believe. Or we do the opposite. We become so desperate to prove that we can be wanted that we throw ourselves into empty sexual experiences with strangers, people we barely know, or people we do not actually like. We want, just for a moment, to feel attractive, beautiful, and desired. But when the rush is over and we lie alone in bed, we are left feeling empty. Or worse, the person we were using wants us to actually care about them, and when we find ourselves unable to do so, we hurt them deeply. Sometimes, out of desperation, we form relationships with people who hurt, betray, use, or control us. We do not want to be alone and, on some level, we think we deserve abuse.

Learning to love our faces, our bodies, our spirits, and ourselves is a journey. The way we see ourselves is built up over years by a variety of forces including messages from family, peers, media, popular culture, religious institutions, and politics, just to name a few. It takes time to discover where self-image comes from, reflect upon it, and ultimately choose what we want to believe about who we are. The work of doing this can be difficult and painful, but it is worth it in the end. We are made to love God, our neighbors, and ourselves. If we do not love ourselves, we are hindered from building healthy and caring relationships with others. In other words, to love God and others well, we must love ourselves. As is written in Ephesians 2: 10, "For we are his handiwork, created in Christ Jesus for the good works that God has prepared in advance, that we should live in them."

Sometimes we are discouraged from loving ourselves by certain beauty ideals upheld by the media and other social institutions. These norms define what it means to be attractive or desirable. They vary across cultures and across time, and they often spring from complicated social and historical roots. Yet consistently, pressure to confirm to a certain body type or facial characteristic is usually a subtle attempt to exert power and control over certain classes of people. Thinness is presented as an ideal in modern Western society in order to sell various products and control people, particularly women, by making them so obsessed with their weight that they have little energy to expend on other matters of empowerment, creativity, or social progress. Muscles are hailed as attractive for men in order to reinforce a culture of men being powerful, dominant, and controlling. This male beauty ideal makes male-dominance in social realms and personal relationships seem enticing rather than oppressive and wrong. Clear skin, and usually light-colored skin, is set as an ideal to sell facial products and make-up while attempting to spread the lie that there is an inborn superiority to people of European descent. Likewise, certain facial features are deemed beautiful in ways that subtly grant favor to groups that typically have them.

Most of us will never fit what the mainstream says is beautiful. Very few of us are genetically programmed to look like models or celebrities. In fact, many models and celebrities who fit society's beauty ideals still suffer from body-related issues such as low self-esteem, chemical dependency, and eating disorders. Many beauty norms are racially and ethnically based so that some people are taught to hate themselves simply for not being white.

We are taught to waste so much energy fixated on ourselves and how we look, and oftentimes we grow envious or resentful of people who seem more beautiful than ourselves. This means we have less energy to gather together in solidarity to make the world a better place. Imagine what would happen if half the money we spent on clothes, make-up, exercise equipment, gym memberships, and beauty products was diverted to ending world hunger. Envision what the world would look like if all the time we spent looking in the mirror and critiquing our looks was spent thinking through strategies for ending modern day slavery, racism, and war. I want to live in a world where people care more about justice than about physical beauty.

Deep down, we must believe that true beauty does not come from how we look, but rather from who we are and how we live. In Mathew 5: 8, we read, "Blessed are the clean of heart, for they will see God." Far more important than shaping our bodies is opening our hearts to God's love so that He may transform us into members of His Body. As we read in 1 Corinthians 12: 27, "Now you are Christ's body, and individually parts of it." Our beauty comes from being united with Christ while maintaining our dignity as individual human beings made and loved by God. We do not grow in beauty by making ourselves conform to an empty social ideal of "looking good." Our inherent beauty is a gift from God. We become even more beautiful when we live with integrity, serve our neighbors, forgive our enemies, spread the good news of God's redeeming love, build justice, and bask in the joy of loving relationships with God and other people.

But feeling ugly and, therefore, unlovable, is a true struggle that cannot be flippantly discarded. The root causes run deep, and therefore the healing must also run deep. Hating the way we look is often connected with the more painful reality of hating our entire selves. When you reflect on who you are, do you only see mistakes and imperfections? Where does this come from? As gay Christians, sometimes we carry deeply internalized shame around our sexual identities. Unfortunately, many religious institutions teach that there is something wrong with loving someone of the same sex, and these messages often sink in even if we fight against them. Self-hatred can also stem from experiences of rejection or bullying. When others hurt us, we sometimes mistakenly believe they do this because we are inherently bad. On some level, we think that we deserve abandonment or abuse. These feelings spiral until we feel as if we are no good and do not belong anywhere. Instead of digging into our pain to figure out what is real and what is deception, it becomes much easier to hate ourselves and our bodies, to blame our unhappiness on the way we look and leave it at that.

But we need to always look for the truth. God made us as and loves us as we are. No one deserves abuse or rejection. God Himself chose to give us love and salvation rather than punishment. As is written in Romans 8: 1, "Hence, now there is no condemnation for those who are in Christ Jesus." Our beauty and our value comes not from how we look or how others treat us. Rather, our beauty and our value comes from our dignity as children of the Most High God. We are created in His image and likeness. As it says in 1 John 3: 1, "See what love the Father has bestowed on us that we may be called the children of God. Yet so we are. The reason the world does not know us is that it did not know him." Thus when others fail to see our beauty or our dignity, we can grow deeper in our connection with Jesus, our Lord, who was also rejected by the world.

In her brilliant work, *The Beauty Myth: How Images of Beauty Are Used Against Women*, author Naomi Wolf (2002) outlines the social construct of beauty and then explains that people can affirm their own worth by loving themselves as full human beings and saying, "I look like myself." Wolf (2002, p. 291) writes, "A woman-loving [Author's note: and also a person-loving] definition of beauty supplants desperation with play, narcissism with self-love, dismemberment with wholeness, absence with presence, stillness with animation. It admits radiance: light coming out of the face and body, rather than a spotlight on the body, dimming the self. It is sexual, various, and surprising. We will be able to see it in others and not be frightened, and able at last to see it in ourselves." We need to look in the mirror and say, *My stomach is precious and beautiful because it is mine. It is a part of me and I love it. My arms are mine, and they allow me to swim and climb and write. My nose is mine and it allows me to smell roses and taste good food. My body is mine, it is part of me, and I love who I am.*

Sometimes we face disabilities or developmental differences that impact how our bodies work. These characteristics and the structure of the spaces around us can pose challenges with moving and navigating the world. But having a disability or a developmental difference also opens opportunities to experience life in unique ways, build new capacities, discover original strengths, and appreciate senses that go underdeveloped in others. There is great power in being different from the mainstream.

Helen Keller, who was herself deaf and blind, is well known as a writer and social justice advocate. For Keller, blindness and deafness were pathways into deeper communion with God and ultimate truth. She wrote, "Our blindness changes not a whit the course of inner realities... If you wish to be something that you are not,— something fine, noble, good,— you shut your eyes and, for one dreamy moment, you are that which you long to be" (Keller, 2003, p. 60). She also wrote, "Men have not heard with their physical sense the tumult of sweet voices above the hills of Judea nor seen the heavenly vision; but millions have listened to that spiritual message through many ages" (Keller, 2003, p. 60).

I do not intend to minimize the suffering or injustice experienced by many people with disabilities. Rather, I want to join the multitude of advocates whose voices point to the intrinsic human dignity of each person. Having a disability does not take away one's capacity or responsibility to learn, grow, believe, build relationships, and work for the common good. At the end of the day, people without disabilities have much to learn from people who have them. Regardless of how our bodies move or work, we are all human, we are all beautiful, and we are all responsible for building a world where everyone is wanted, everyone is valued, and everyone belongs.

People face a deep and often painful struggle when they feel that aspects of their bodies do not correspond with their true gender identities. Sometimes we see people in the mirror we do not recognize. We wish our chests were flat instead of curvy or curvy instead of flat. We wish for internal or external genitalia. We wish for our facial features to grow in either delicacy or boldness. It sometimes feels wrong to sit with our own flesh, and we wish to live in a body that feels like home. And when we take steps to make our bodies look or feel right, sometimes the people around us do not understand. Out of fear or ignorance, they might sometimes belittle, mock, reject, or hurt us.

If this is your struggle, I want you to know that you are not alone. You may not see them every day, but many people hold gender identities that do not match what they were assigned at birth, and many of these people feel like certain parts of their bodies do not fit right. Wherever you are in the process of discovering who you are and how you feel about your body, God is with you. As is written in Joshua 1: 9, "I command you: be firm and steadfast! Do not fear nor be dismayed, for the Lord, your God, is with you wherever you go." Open up to God, and He will help you understand who you are and where to go from here. Maybe in time you will be interested and able to make changes to your body through hormones or surgery. Maybe someday you will find ways to live out your true gender and make peace with your body as it is.

In the throes of the struggle, I encourage you to pray from your heart and reach out to others who are understanding and supportive. Find community groups with other people who live outside of the cisgender binary. Read books and articles that advocate for body love, free gender expression, truth, and justice. Volunteer for educational and activist projects that build gender equality, inclusivity, understanding, and peace. Try to hold onto the things you like about your body. Even though there parts that feel wrong, are there still things you can do with your body that bring you joy? Does it make you happy to jump, to walk in the rain, to roll down a grassy hill? Do you enjoy the feeling of a hot shower or the sun on your skin? Do you cherish the taste of ice cream or the smell of lilacs? Are you thankful for eyes that let you gaze upon art, meadows, and the sunset? What aspects of your body bring goodness to your life?

I do not want to minimize anyone's challenges or tell anyone to ignore their suffering. Rather, I simply hope we can all find moments of peace to help carry us through the path ahead. Once again, you need not be alone on the journey. Even if you are at a stage of life when no one around you understands, God is with you. He will help you learn who you are and how to love yourself by the power of His great love for you. As we read in Zephaniah 3: 17, "The LORD, your God, is in your midst, a mighty savior; he will rejoice over you with gladness, and renew you in his love, he will sing joyfully because of you."

As you take steps to live out and love your gender identity, your abilities, your racial and ethnic background, and the shape of your unique body, people of the world may sometimes react with judgement, hatred, or violence. Such is often the response to courage and truth. As Jesus says in John 15: 18, "If the world hates you, realize that it hated me first." Once again we read in 2 Timothy 4: 12, "In fact, all who want to live religiously in Christ Jesus will be persecuted." Notice that this text does not state that all people who claim to be Christians will be persecuted, but rather those who *live religiously in Christ Jesus.* If we want to, we can be Christians who live miserable lives of petty conformity. We can study all the social norms and rigidly control how we act, what we say, and what we believe. We can hide the truth of who we are and make all our choices out of the desire to be safe, comfortable, and relatively well-liked.

But this is not the path opened to us by Christ. In his time on earth, Jesus was a revolutionary who boldly walked in righteousness and truth, yet he did so with a spirit of absolute peace, love, and humility. This is the mind-blowing revelation of Christ, that true power is not found in war and dominance, but in love and self-sacrifice. When people hurt and reject us, we need to persist in mercy and truth, for this is our Christian duty, this is the way of the cross, and this is how we witness to God's infinite and redeeming love. As we read in 1 Peter 3: 14-17:

But even if you should suffer because of righteousness, blessed are you. Do not be afraid or terrified with fear of them, but sanctify Christ as Lord in your hearts. Always be ready to give an explanation to anyone who asks you for a reason for your hope, but do it with gentleness and reverence, keeping your conscience clear, so that, when you are maligned, those who defame your good conduct in Christ may themselves be put to shame. For it is better to suffer for doing good, if that be the will of God, than for doing evil.

I am not advising you to accept abuse. Rather, we need to protect ourselves, set healthy boundaries, and hold people accountable for their unjust actions while still holding the love of Christ supreme in our hearts. If someone says something cruel, we can respond by removing ourselves from the situation, speaking up to them, or asking others for help. We can do all these things while praying for the person who spoke cruelly, *Dear God, show them the error of their thinking and their ways. Help them to know your truth and your love more deeply.*

If we are physically or sexually assaulted, we must seek help and ask God to heal our bodies, hearts, and souls. Trauma like this changes us, and we need support from loved ones, medical providers, and community members to make it through. Sometimes we blame ourselves when we are hurt so brutally, but we must remember that absolutely no one deserves to be assaulted. Whether we press legal charges or not, we can eventually make meaning of our experiences by reaching out to others who suffer in similar ways or working to stop these atrocities from happening again. In time, we can open our hearts in prayer: *God, please heal whatever anger, pain, or brokenness moved this person to hurt me. Stop them from hurting others, and let the cycle of violence stop with me. Please take the anger, fear, powerlessness, and self-loathing that I feel in this moment and fill me with mercy, love, peace, and a righteous zeal for justice. I believe that You will prevail in all things. Through this experience, transform me into an advocate for healing and goodness in Your world.*

Once again, if we do not love ourselves, it will be nearly impossible to live out love for our neighbors and enemies. Ultimately, we must open our eyes to see that life is a gift from God. We must rejoice in all the good things we can do with our bodies, our minds, and our hearts. We need to let God heal whatever causes us hurt and shame. We need to let God see us, know us, and love us. In God's love, we learn that we are good and lovable. As we read in Psalm 147: 2-3, "The LORD rebuilds Jerusalem, gathers the dispersed of Israel, heals the brokenhearted, binds up their wounds." He makes us whole again so that we can be fountains of love for others, for God's love will always flow into the world through us. Thus we must turn to God and pray the words of Jeremiah 17: 14: "Heal me, LORD, that I may be healed; save me, that I may be saved, for it is you whom I praise."

We need to seek healing not only for our own good, but also for the good of others. Self-loathing often devolves into hating others. Growing up, I was fatter than my peers, I had an effeminate voice, and I loved My Little Ponies decades before it was popular for boys to do such a thing. Naturally, I was bullied by certain peers, called names, excluded from some group activities, and generally perceived as being strange and different. Many of the people who were cruel to me were boys who the world considered to be handsome, popular, and likeable. They were physically attractive, athletic, charismatic, and funny. I survived those years with the loving support of family, the friendship of wonderful teachers, and the grace of God.

As I grew up, I harbored a great deal of anger toward men who were traditionally attractive or popular. In time, I realized that I had learned to associate beauty with cruelty, popularity with meanness, and charisma with abusive power. I wanted to protect myself from beautiful people because I automatically feared them. Deep down, I also envied their beauty and their easy-going social grace. Whenever I saw a beautiful, respected man, my initial reaction was fear and dislike. I did not see the person in front of me, but rather some phantom I created in my own head.

Once I realized what was going on for me, I came to understand that I was not seeing as God sees. As is written in 1 Samuel 16: 7 B, "Not as man sees does God see, because man sees the appearance but the LORD looks into the heart." God helped me overcome my harsh, shallow judgements so that I could perceive people as full human beings who were made, saved, and loved by God. I learned that everyone, pretty or ugly, short or tall, fat or thin or somewhere in between, absolutely everyone has a deep need for love and for God. God gave me the grace to see that the people who hurt me in childhood must have been broken by some pain in their own lives. I was merely a target for their frustration, their anger, their need to experience some sort of power. God helped me see that Jesus came to earth, died, and rose for all of us, no matter what we look like, what we have done, or what we plan to do. Hating or judging only takes us away from the peace that can only be found in God's love.

When we let go of the heavy burdens of self-hate and judgment, we are able to open our hearts more deeply and honestly to others. We no longer need to push people away out of fear of rejection, and we no longer need to hold onto the pain of the past. We are set free to pray for those who hurt us and let the rest go. Each day becomes an opportunity to receive God's love and share it ever more widely and deeply with the world. Rather than obsessing about ourselves and fearing our neighbors, we can channel our energy into serving our friends, families, and communities. And we can open our hearts to romantic love when it comes our way with an honest courage about who we are, what we feel, who we want, and how we expect to be treated.

The truth is that however you look, you are beautiful because you are a child of God. As is written in Galatians 3: 26, "For through faith you are all children of God in Christ Jesus." Is there any beauty greater than belonging to the family of God and the Body of Christ? God gave us hearts that yearn for love. There will be opportunities to live out love in our lives. We just need to be open and ready when they come along, and we can start by loving God and loving ourselves today.

The world needs people of faith who courageously profess that we are all beautiful children of God. When we love ourselves as we are today, we take a stand for truth and justice. We become pioneers who lead the way for those around us. We denounce the lies that we need to look a certain way to be beautiful, handsome, attractive, or lovable.

Once again, learning to love yourself is a journey, and some people have more obstacles than others. There are many dangerous traps related to bodies, health, and eating. We might eat too much or too little, purge through vomiting or laxatives, exercise too much, hurt ourselves physically to control emotional pain, or think about suicide. If any of these things are happening in your life, please reach out for help. Talk to a family member, close friend, trusted teacher, mentor, or pastor. If the first person you tell does not react well, tell someone else. Connect with a counselor and, if you are seriously thinking about ending your life, go to a nearby hospital. You are precious and the world needs to hear the testimony of how you overcome what you are going through right now through the grace of God.

As you walk your journey, here are some other things you can do:

- Think positively about yourself. Write lists of ten things you love to do, ten things you want to try, ten things you like about yourself, and ten things you have accomplished. It is often easy to list negative things about ourselves and difficult to come up with positive things, but this exercise can be deeply healing! Write the lists. If you struggle to come up with ideas, pray about it and ask for suggestions from trusted family and friends.

- Replace negative thoughts about yourself with positive ones as they come up throughout the day. Talk back to yourself. If you think, *I'm so fat,* or, *My nose is too big,* or, *When will these zits ever go away,* quickly reply with, *I look like myself,* or, *Look at this sexy beast in the mirror,* or, *I have beautiful eyes,* or, *I can't wait to go dancing later, even if it's just in the living room.* You get to choose what you think. When it feels like your thoughts are stuck in the same rut, ask God to help you move your mind in a different direction. Also, try writing the negative thoughts down on one side of a piece of paper. Next, respond to each statement by writing positive thoughts on the other side of the page. Putting thoughts down in concrete writing takes them out of the murky depths of the mind.

-Learn new healthy coping skills. Sometimes we cling to negativity about how we look or control our eating in order to cope with the pain and stress of life. If we learn other skills, such as taking deep breaths, drawing, distracting ourselves with fun activities, taking walks, praying, reading, writing, or talking with others about our problems, this helps us cope in ways that are less harmful and more productive.

- Talk about your progress with trusted family members or friends. You are not alone in the struggle. Many of us do not like how we look and sometimes struggle with feeling unlovable. Talk with other people who accept you as you are. Support each other. Ask each other, *Why do we struggle with seeing ourselves as not good enough? What is the root cause of this, and where do we go from here?*

-Practice affirmations. Say short, positive statements about yourself and your dreams out loud over and over again until you believe them. For example, you could say, "I am beautiful and strong… God loves me… I am sexy… There is a person out there for me to love… God wants me and I want me… My life matters…" Words are powerful. Write your affirmations down on note cards. Hang them up by a mirror or place them on your desk so you remember to say them throughout the day.

-Meditate on Scripture. Repeat verses of scripture to yourself over and over, and let them fill you with strength and hope. God's word transforms us and enables us to see the world through God's eyes. Scripture draws our hearts, minds, and wills closer to God, who is love.

Furthermore, it is sometimes helpful to remember that looks are just one piece of romantic chemistry, and different people are attracted to different qualities. Some people like guys with six pack abs and some people like guys with cuddly, teddy bear tummies. Some people like girls with willowy figures and some people like girls with soft, generous curves. Some people like blue eyes, some people like brown eyes, and most people care more about the passion in a person's eyes than the color of the irises. Looks are often a factor in feelings of love and lust, but there are so many other elements to consider. Healthy, loving relationships are built on compatible senses of humor, lifestyles, personalities, values, goals, and beliefs. We fall in love with entire human beings, not soulless bodies. As we shift focus away from how we look, we pay more attention to living with integrity as disciples of Jesus. To see others deeply, we need to see ourselves deeply; and to love others deeply, we need to love ourselves deeply.

We need to love our bodies and our lives. God will help us get there if we let Him.

Love,

Aaron

FOR WHEN YOU ARE READY TO FACE YOUR DEMONS, REJECT IDOLS, AND TURN AWAY FROM FALSE GODS

"But when he prays about his goods or marriage or children, he is not ashamed to address the thing without a soul. And for vigor he invokes the powerless; and for life he entreats the dead; and for aid he beseeches the wholly incompetent, and about travel, something that cannot even walk."

- Wisdom 13: 17-18

"You have been told, O man, what is good, and what the LORD requires of you: only to do the right and to love goodness, and to walk humbly with your God."

- Micah 6: 8

Dear Sister, Dear Brother, Dear Friend,

We were made for love and freedom. We were created to love God, love others, and love ourselves. To live in peace with our own nature, we must hold God at the center of our lives. God is truth, mercy, goodness, and love itself. Our dreams, thoughts, words, and actions must be rooted in God and the mission She gives us to bring joy to the world.

When we make something that is not God the center of our lives, that thing becomes an idol or a false god. In Exodus 20: 2-3, God says, "I, the LORD, am your God, who brought you out of the land of Egypt, that place of slavery. You shall not have other gods besides me." For the people of Israel in the ancient world, the great temptation was to worship pagan deities represented by objects made of stone or wood. Worshiping these false gods did nothing except turn people away from the one true God. The pain and foolishness of such a choice is captured in the words of Wisdom 13: 17-18: "But when he prays about his goods or marriage or children, he is not ashamed to address the thing without a soul. And for vigor he invokes the powerless; and for life he entreats the dead; and for aid he beseeches the wholly incompetent, and about travel, something that cannot even walk." St. Paul gives a clear and gentle warning in 1 Corinthians 10: 14 when he writes, "Therefore, my beloved, avoid idolatry."

In the modern day, people may be less tempted to worship pagan deities made of wood or stone, yet there are still countless idols that people use to replace God. Idols can take the form of actions, habits, desires, people, or material things. Some of these false gods actively damage our own lives or hurt others, such as drugs or excessive alcohol use, irresponsible sexual behavior, materialism, or selfishness. Such idols become personal demons or temptations that actively pull us from God and loving communion with our neighbors. But idols can also be good things, actions, dreams, or even attachments to people that become corrupted when we treat them as more important than God. Financial security, ambition to do good things with one's life, or a beloved person are all good things worthy of pursuit, time, energy, and commitment. But in the midst of our work, our goals, and our relationships, we must realize that everything we do is for the love of God and because God calls us to love others. If we forget that, we will run out of energy to do good by cutting ourselves off from God, who is the source of everything. Idols make promises of happiness, fulfillment, or peace that they cannot keep. When we make idols the center of our lives, we miss opportunities to live fully in love and truth because we have chosen paths that do not lead to God.

We all carry brokenness from pain that we have endured and witnessed. There are times when we feel alone, unloved, unwanted, hated, used, belittled, or ignored. God wants to hold and heal us in our brokenness. She wants to give us peace that the world cannot give. Yet sometimes it seems easier to have our needs met, soothe our anxieties, escape our fears, or satisfy our desires by choosing something that is not God. Rather than turning to God for purpose, joy, and healing, it seems easier, faster, or simply more in line with the crowd to choose another way. We seek a quick fix that will help us escape pain or make us feel good, satisfied, or valued in the moment. Other times, we feel as if we do not deserve God's love, and so we do things we know will hurt us to punish ourselves or confirm deeply held beliefs that we are no good. We cheat ourselves of our true inheritance as children of God. But if we are honest with ourselves, we know deep down when we are on the wrong path because there is always a yearning deep inside for something more. We yearn for God.

How do we break chains of poor choices and escape our demons? We must turn to God. We must pray and allow grace to transform our hearts. We must open our souls to God's limitless forgiveness so that we might forgive others and forgive ourselves.

We often find God's healing grace through relationship with one another. We lean on friends and family who help us grow into our best selves. We help each other carry on through suffering and hold each other up rather than running away from the pain. We face our demons and realize that God will conquer them for us as long as we let Her.

Read on and you will see that a large part of this letter deals with common demons that people face and ways to overcome them, but first I want to share some stories of my personal idols. I do this to show that our spiritual struggles are unique and sometimes we need to do some digging to discover how we are being led astray.

One false idol I struggle with is a romanticized dream of falling in love and getting married. When I thought I was straight, I had grandiose notions of falling in love with a woman and getting married. After realizing I was gay and coming out, I had similar dreams of falling in love with a man and getting married. In both cases, this dream started out as an innocent and noble goal for my life. It is good to find and build romantic love. It is good for two people who love each other to commit themselves to one another in marriage and start a family together. However, what started out for me as a happy fantasy eventually became an unhealthy obsession. I did not enjoy dating because I was not falling in love with anyone. Without realizing it, I came to believe that my life would not truly begin until I got married. From there I came to think that I had no love in my life whatsoever because I was single. I lost sight of every blessing God had given me, including the tender and devoted love of family and friends, meaningful work, and the joy of reading books, hiking, eating good food, and simply being alive. I even seemed to forget the most important part of life, which was enjoying a loving relationship with God. I sulked and listened to sad music and made myself miserable because I lacked one particular object that I wanted, which was a relationship with a spouse.

Once I realized that wanting a loving partner had become a false god, I was able to give this dream to God in prayer. I asked Her to transform me and show me how I could love the people in my life better today. Over time, romantic love and marriage returned to being a hopeful dream that was part of my balanced life rather than an obsessive need. God helped me learn and grow through this experience. She set me free to enjoy my life and make meaning in every day.

Another idol I struggle with is over-prioritizing my professional career. For years, I tortured myself wondering over and over again what job I should pursue. I thought I needed to find the perfect job that would use all of my talents and fulfill every purpose for which I was created. Over time, I bounced from position to position. There were things I liked and disliked with every new role. Nothing was ever good enough. I went from being a preschool teacher to a barista to a youth group facilitator to a janitor to a counselor to a hospital social worker. I prayed and prayed to find the perfect job that would satisfy the desires in my heart. Somewhere along the way, God opened my eyes to see that I was trying to make my job the center of meaning in my life rather than God. It is good to pursue meaningful work and use one's gifts for the greater good, but we must do this without burying ourselves in dissatisfaction and pressure. God helped me see that we are all commanded to love God, love our neighbors, and love ourselves, and there are countless opportunities to accomplish these goals in any job. If we ask, God will show us how to make meaning in all areas of our lives, including at work, in relationships, in church communities, in volunteer roles, in artistic endeavors, and in contact with strangers we encounter in day to day life. In my pride, I had been searching for a clear and vibrant mission that I could hold up as proof that my life was important. God helped me see that I am important and meaningful because I am made in Her image and She loves me. I do not need a perfect job. If I open myself to God, She will help me to discover and shape meaning in every moment of every day.

There are some classic idols that tempt most of us to various degrees throughout our lives. These include wealth, unholy power, lust, rigid moral legality, and worldly praise. It is important to look at these closely to realize how we can turn away from our demons and give ourselves completely to God. I do not think the journey is about hating ourselves for breaking rules, but rather deepening in understanding of how we can live in freedom, truth, goodness, and joy.

One idol we might chase is wealth and the accumulation of material possessions. There is no denying the value of a nice home, an expensive car, a hefty bank account, and all the trappings of a comfortable life. These items hold the allure of security and stand firm in our modern world as symbols of success. Many who survive hard times or poverty yearn to protect themselves and their loved ones from hardship, and this is a noble goal. Pursuing financial responsibility and providing for one's family are great virtues. Likewise, we must enjoy the bounty of the earth and the fruit of human creativity if we are to achieve balance and remain grateful for all God has given us. God wants us to be grateful for life, cherish beauty, and support robust economies where people thrive in community with one another.

However, a serious problem emerges when accumulating wealth and stuff becomes more important than loving people and God. The truth is that the earth has limited resources. For our planet to survive and for all people everywhere to get what they need, each person must be committed to using resources and goods responsibly. It is good to enjoy what you have, take what we need, and share the rest. It is not good to take and take and take for oneself without caring about one's neighbors or the rest of Creation.

Why is it so tempting to take more than our fair share? Sometimes it feels good to have a lot of things. Sometimes we crave the security of having much more than we really need. Many people wish to be admired and think they can get this kind of attention by wearing expensive clothes, living in a big house on the water, or driving a deluxe convertible. This hunger to be noticed and liked can be especially strong in gay people and other oppressed groups who have been taught all their lives that they are less valuable than others. When we put material goods above God and service to our neighbors, we fail to recognize the demands of justice and human dignity. We were made to be more than things that collect other things. Our value comes not from what we own or what others think of us, but rather from our identity as children of God. We were made to love God and care for one another.

Scripture is full of messages compelling us to place love and God above material things. Mammon is an Aramaic word for wealth, and in Luke 16: 13, Jesus says, "No servant can serve two masters. He will either hate one and love the other, or be devoted to one and despise the other. You cannot serve God and mammon." Jesus compels us to choose who we will follow and how we will spend our time in this life. Will we focus on our own security and comfort, or will we live for God? Jesus says in Matthew 6: 19-21, "Do not store up for yourselves treasures on earth, where moth and decay destroy, and thieves break in and steal. But store up treasures in heaven, where neither moth nor decay destroy, nor thieves break in and steal. For where your treasure is, there also will your heart be." We must place our hearts in God who is love, for She is our greatest treasure and we are Hers.

Jesus says in Matthew 5: 3, "Blessed are the poor in spirit, for theirs is the kingdom of heaven." Much has been written about this verse over the centuries. People wonder, is Jesus telling us to be poor? To be clear, I do not think God wants anyone to live in the fear, hunger, deprivation, sickness, squalor, and injustice that is true poverty. The state of poverty exists because our world is broken by sin, especially the sin of some people hoarding rather than sharing the goods of the earth and the works of human hands. When Jesus calls the "poor in spirit" blessed, I believe he is calling us to a radical dependence on God. I believe Jesus wants us to see material goods as gifts from God. These gifts are not ends in themselves. They allow us to thrive and provide us with opportunities to love and serve. Our homes should not be fortresses where we hide from the world; they should be hubs of healing and love for our neighbors. Our cars should not be chariots that take us where we want to go; they should be means to transport ourselves and others to places of healing, learning, service, worship, recreation, mission, and play. The clothes we wear and books we read and knick-knacks that become little parts of our lives should not be objects that exist merely for our own pleasure; they should be tools and symbols that inspire us to be more loving, creative, and fruitful people. Our bank accounts should not exist merely for the well-being of ourselves and our families; they should be shared in a balanced and responsible way for the well-being of all.

If we depend on God and use all we have for bringing about justice, we will have a healthy relationship with material goods. If we work hard and share the fruits of our labor in a spirit of generosity, we will live in the peace offered by Jesus in Matthew 6: 25-26: "Therefore I tell you, do not worry about your life, what you will eat or drink, or about your body, what you will wear. Is not life more than food and the body more than clothing? Look at the birds in the sky; they do not sow or reap, they gather nothing into barns, yet your heavenly Father feeds them. Are not you more important than they?"

Unholy power is another idol that is closely tied with wealth because wealth and power feed each other. Power can be defined as having influence on oneself, other people, the community, or the world. Power is the ability to make or stifle change. Thirsting after power for its own sake is a serious temptation for those who experience the fear and degradation of weakness. We live in a world that strips many of their power by denying rights, leveling threats, enacting violence, and whispering in a thousand voices, *You are not good enough as you are.* God wants to fill us with the power of Her love through the Holy Spirit, who is capable of moving mountains and raising the dead. As Christians, we are the Body of Christ alive in the world today. God wants to give us power so that we may use it to do good.

So when does power become unholy, a false idol rather than God's gift? Power becomes unholy when we seek it for our own satisfaction, for the thrill of telling others what to do, think, or believe, for the rush of controlling other people's lives. When we seek power over others to escape from the pain of our own weakness, we turn our backs on the mission of love which is the purpose of God-given power. In addition, Christian power is often completely different from worldly power. The world's understanding of power focuses on control over others and aggrandizement of the self, often at the expense of someone else. Dictators are powerful; corporate leaders are powerful; politicians in seats of decision-making authority are powerful; celebrities with millions of fans hanging on their every word are powerful. For Christians, the most powerful moment in all time took place when Jesus overcame sin and death through humiliation, torture, and death on a cross. Jesus's power to give us eternal life came through his self-sacrifice, his suffering, his death, and his resurrection. Despite incredible fear, he bore it all with unconditional love for everyone, including his own tormentors and the greatest sinners of every age. Nothing is more powerful than Jesus's mercy as he hangs from the cross and speaks the words, "…Father, forgive them, they know not what they do…" (Luke 23: 34).

When we live under the weight of our own crosses, the world tells us these are our greatest moments of humiliation, suffering, and weakness. But the truth is that when people hate us, call us names, mock our voices, criticize our hair, call us prudes, call us whores, strike us, beat us up, belittle us, or persecute us in any way, we have the choice to let these moments connect us deeply with the mysterious and saving power of Jesus' crucifixion. Each insult is a nail in our hands and feet, each blow a stab from our own crowns of thorns. We must never hide in shame but always survive and struggle with Christ to endure suffering and change the world. We must forgive those who persecute us, for they too are broken and hurting. In moments of humiliation and pain, we are indeed weak. But as St. Paul says in 2 Corinthians 12: 10, "Therefore, I am content with weaknesses, insults, hardships, persecutions, and constraints, for the sake of Christ; for when I am weak, then I am strong."

The world will tell us that suffering and weakness is defeat. As Christians, we must believe that when we surrender in weakness, God will transform our suffering into triumph and strength. God meets us where we are, holds us there, sanctifies our suffering, and works in it to bring greater redemption to the world. This place of pain is where miracles happen.

I am not saying that we should be masochists, seek suffering, ignore oppression, or accept abuse. That would be like believing that Jesus's story ends after his suffering and death. But the story goes on. Jesus rises, and we must rise with him. We must face our tormentors, forgive them, demand change, and fight for justice. But Christ's resurrection and ours means that the suffering is not meaningless. If we invite God to help us carry our crosses, we no longer need to dwell in hopelessness and misery. The joy of the Holy Spirit is not dependent on worldly circumstances or feelings. She is an eternal wellspring of hope who moves us to take step after step in building up the Kingdom of God whether the world sees us as weak or strong. Jesus gives this promise in Matthew 11: 28-30: "Come to me, all you who labor and are burdened, and I will give you rest. Take my yoke upon you and learn from me, for I am meek and humble of heart; and you will find rest for yourselves. For my yoke is easy, and my burden light."

If you feel today as if you have no power, give yourself to God. Give God your suffering, dreams, fears, courage, and love. Open your eyes to opportunities for building community with other people, whether this be through a church, school, club, team, workplace, library, community center, evening class, bible study, or volunteer job. Each of us is a part of the Body of Christ alive in the world today. We cannot do anything on our own. We need God and we need each other. If you surrender to God, She will guide you to good work that needs doing, surround you with people to care about, and fill you with the strength you need to carry on. Whether you feel powerful or weak, trust in God and let God be your strength at all times.

Lust is a false idol that is often praised as one of the greatest goods in the gay community. It is absolutely vital to remember that sex is created by God to be joyous, thrilling, and very, very good. Sex is meant to be exciting, fun, and cherished by those who share it. It has the power to be an intense expression of love. The Song of Solomon in the Bible is filled with passionate verses about longing, intimacy, and the joy of connecting body and soul with another person. Sexuality is the fire that holds a couple together, and therefore it is one foundation of creating a family.

Sometimes we are tempted to lust, which is the pursuit of sex without love. There are times when we just want to feel good and not think about how sexual acts impact others or ourselves. Sometimes we are lonely and yearn to experience a sense of connection with another person, even if it is only physical or even if the other person is committed to someone else. Maybe we want to use the pleasure of sex to chase away something that plagues us, such as sadness, guilt, or emptiness. Maybe we yearn to feel wanted, valuable, or loved, and casual or illicit sex makes us feel that way, if only for a little while. Maybe we feel pressure to get experience or prove we are sexy, and so we seek sex just to be like everyone else. In the gay community, there is a lot of pressure to be sexually attractive, feel good in the moment, and do what we feel like without thinking too much about it. As gay Christians, a lot of loneliness, shame, and feelings of being unlovable often spring from homophobic messages we receive from certain faith communities. This double-sided pressure to seek sex without love often leads individuals to make irresponsible decisions in terms of sex and relationships, which leads to hordes of people being betrayed or used by various partners. People who get hurt then go around and hurt other people in dating and in bed, and this leads to a tragic state of affairs.

When we use sex exclusively to make ourselves feel good, experience power, or meet our own needs, we turn our partner or partners into objects who exist merely for our own satisfaction. We deny the human dignity of the other person. At the same time, even if we try to remove love from sex, it remains deeply intimate by its very nature. Therefore, when we have sex with strangers or people we cannot fully commit to, our bodies make promises that we never intend to keep. Furthermore, lust lies at the root of many evils far more insidious other than sex without love. Lust combined with thirst for unholy power results in human trafficking, sexual exploitation of youth, pornography, child pornography, sexual assault, and sexual abuse. These painful realities are rooted in the desire to satisfy cravings for power and sexual release by hurting, using, and dehumanizing others.

As humans, we are graced with the gift of sexuality. With this grace comes a sacred duty to love others and ourselves, to respect our bodies and those of others as temples of the Holy Spirit of God. Sex does not inherently pollute or denigrate our bodies. Rather, we are called to live our sexual lives in ways that bring joy into the world, not sorrow; fulfillment, not emptiness; union, not discord; ecstasy, not pain; freedom, not slavery. I encourage you to embrace your sexuality as a gift. Ask God to show you the best way to live out your sex drive given your current stage of life, and be honest with yourself about where She leads you. Read through Scripture and talk with good, wise, trusted people who truly want the best for you. It is fun to have crushes and attractions. It is thrilling to get to know the beautiful body of a person you are dating. It is ecstatic to make love with the love of one's life. Sometimes it all gets very confusing. We do not always know where we should draw our boundaries or even how to figure it out. Should we create lists of rules for when to proceed to the next sexual activity? Should these rules be based on length of time, feelings, or commitments? Should we seek to live in the Spirit of truth and let things flow and develop naturally? If we do this, how do we know if our actions are flowing in the path intended by the Holy Spirit or diverted by waves of lust?

Take time to ponder these questions in prayer, and know that there is absolutely no rush to come to any conclusions. You must take the time to decide in good conscience what you believe is right, and you must talk with any potential partner about their beliefs and desires. It is important to consider what sex means to you and what it means to the other person. Many painful misunderstandings happen simply because people do not talk about what they are doing before they do it. Does this person think that sex means the two of you love each other, or not? Does this person think that sex means you are dating each other exclusively, or not? Does this other person think that sex is important and special, or not? It is also absolutely vital that whoever you connect with gives full and unambiguous consent. Whether you are holding hands, kissing, making out, or getting naked together, you should both understand where the other person is coming from and you should communicate openly and honestly that this is what you both want. No one should ever pressure another person to do something sexually that they do not want to do. Sex should be lived out in joy and freedom, not fear and abuse.

So ask God, how should I live out my sexuality today? How can I love another person best with my body, heart, and soul? If I feel an intense desire to connect with someone tonight but there are no potential soulmates on the horizon, what should I do? Where should I draw the line with this current relationship or future relationships? How can I honor my body and their body as Temples of the Holy Spirit? How am I called to love today?

As you ponder these important questions, remember that sex is made to be amazing, joyful, and good. It is made to hold families together and bring life into the world. When things get complicated, confusing, or hurtful, try to step back and thank God for the amazing gifts of your body and your libido. Being a sexual being can be frustrating and lonely, but it can also be exhilarating and tender. If times are hard now, trust that the seasons will eventually change. Give the fires of your heart and body to God. She will guide you to the good things She has in store for you.

In works about idols and demons, one would expect to find words about wealth, power, and lust. But some idols are more subtle and come disguised as false virtue. One such idol is that of approaching morality through rigid legality. Rather than living a life of love, sometimes we build our lives around a mirthless set of rules and beliefs that become a system of false gods. This can be especially tempting for gay Christians. If we experience deeply internalized guilt or shame, we may want desperately to escape it by pretending to be models of so-called "perfect Christians." Rather than surrendering to Christ and letting him heal us, we seek to conform our behavior to moral laws. We hope that "being good" will make up for past sins or somehow compensate for the mistaken belief that there is something inherently wrong with us for being gay. We act the way we think is right, but our hearts are not in it. We try to earn our own salvation rather than accepting redemption as a gift from Christ, and we make idols of the laws we seek to follow.

In chapter two of Mark's gospel, some of Jesus' disciples are criticized by religious leaders of the time for picking heads of grain on the Sabbath day and therefore violating rules that prohibit working on what should be a day of rest. In Mark 2: 27, we read, "Then he [Jesus] said to them, 'The Sabbath was made for man, not man for the Sabbath." Jesus calls us to open our eyes and realize that moral laws are not made to be ends in and of themselves. Rather, God's commandments are given to us to help us live more deeply in the ways of love. We make false gods of our limited human notions if we think that we are always right, that we have all the answers to every question, that we are perfect if we follow a narrow set of rules. In so doing, we disconnect ourselves from the one, true, living God.

This approach to life has many devastating consequences. First of all, it is highly arrogant and, therefore, destructive. God speaks through Her prophet in Isaiah 55: 9: "As high as the heavens are above the earth, so high are my ways above your ways and my thoughts above your thoughts." If we trust in our own human answers to everything, we subject ourselves to human flaws like prejudice, exploitation, and lack of any vision that could possibly encompass all of reality. As human beings, we cannot fully grasp the eternal mysteries of God and the universe. We cannot even fully grasp our own lives or those of people around us. We see little pieces, usually one or two at a time. This does not mean we should give up the search. Rather, we must be committed to continually growing deeper and deeper in knowing God and Her ways, in learning how to love others and ourselves day by day.

Another problem with living a rigid, legalistic lifestyle is that it binds us to slavery rather than setting us free to live as children of God. In his letter to the Galatians, St. Paul consistently urges the Christian community to receive grace through the new covenant in Christ by releasing themselves from bondage to certain elements of the Mosaic law. The words of Galatians 5: 1 still resonate with us today: "For freedom Christ set us free; so stand firm and do not submit again to the yoke of slavery." God is alive in us and calls us to live in the freedom of Christ. We are not made to be cold, judgmental copies of each other. We are made to be ourselves, to be people saved in Christ, to be unique children of God, to live in the freedom of the Holy Spirit. St. Paul continues in Galatians 5: 22-23, "In contrast, the fruit of the Spirit is love, joy, peace, patience, kindness, generosity, faithfulness, gentleness, self-control. Against such there is no law."

I am not saying we should abandon traditional morality and do whatever we want. The point is this: when choosing how to live our lives, we must go beyond conforming to predetermined customs and open ourselves to the Holy Spirit of the living God. We need to let ourselves be moved by compassion. We need to think creatively about how to solve the unique problems of our lives, our communities, and our world. We need to dream with a vision that embraces goodness and celebrates diversity. We need to believe that faith in God is more than following a set of rules or adhering to a list of beliefs. Faith in God means living a life of love. It means listening to the words God speaks to us in every moment. It means giving ourselves over, body, heart, mind, and soul, to love itself. It means choosing to be absolutely alive and free to do the will of God and to live in joy. As it says in Micah 6: 8, "You have been told, O man, what is good, and what the LORD requires of you: only to do the right and to love goodness, and to walk humbly with your God."

Another false idol is that of worldly praise or, in other words, wanting to be liked by others. Those of us who have felt rejected by the world often feel a deep need to belong. We want to feel wanted, and we are sometimes willing to do whatever it takes to be perceived as good, beautiful, handsome, sexy, funny, or popular. These desires can be especially strong for gay Christians who feel they do not fully belong within any community. Sometimes we feel too gay for mainstream Christian groups and too Christian for mainstream gay groups.

There is nothing wrong with enjoying the warmth and admiration of others. Healthy relationships are built on mutual respect and kindness. We must learn from one another and express gratitude for one another. Problems come when we focus our energy on doing things that get us positive feedback from others. If we live honestly and rightly, there will be some who approve of us and others who do not. It is liberating to commit ourselves to God, live in truth, and not worry too much about what other people think. We must seek God's approval first and trust that She made us exactly as She intended. If someone does not like what we do or who we are, we must listen to see if there is something we need to learn from them, pray about it, and move on. With God on our side, we have nothing to fear.

Sometimes we sacrifice our values, hide what we believe in, or ignore things that are wrong in order to fit in with the crowd. More subtly, sometimes we do good works not to share love but rather to bring glory to ourselves. When we fall into these traps, we distract ourselves from the people we are called to be. We hesitate to reach out to people who are rejected because we do not want to be rejected with them. We forget that Jesus ate with tax collectors, sinners, Pharisees, fishermen, and sex workers. Jesus shared bread with everyone and calls us to do the same. Other times we might exhaust ourselves with exercise, starve ourselves with diets, or hurl insults at the mirror because we never feel good enough. Or we hide our emotions and our opinions out of fear that they will be mocked. We forget what it is like to be moved by love to do good because our good deeds are always forced. Our world shrinks until we become the center and everything we do is intended to reflect on ourselves in a positive way. The world becomes just another mirror. There is no room in such a small world for God or the wild joy She intends for us.

I implore you to allow God to set you free. Let go of anxiety about whether or not you are liked by others. Rather, seek God and Her approval. Follow the example of Christ and reach out to everyone in love. Use the strengths, talents, and beliefs God has given you to do your part to build up the Kingdom of God. Love your body not because of what it looks like but because of what you can do as an embodied spirit loved and saved by God. If you can run, run for the sheer joy of the wind in your face. If you can sing, sing praises to our loving Creator. If you can move, move yourself to a group of people that need your help. If you live this way, you will find plenty of people who like you and plenty who will try to tear you down. Listen to the good and pray for those who try to hurt you. Never let anyone steal your joy. Embrace the freedom Christ rose from the dead to give you. Step forward as a child of the one true God. Become fully alive this very minute, and never look back.

And so, my friend, perhaps you are reading this letter because something has ensnared you and you want to be free. Let me testify that God's power to save is unstoppable. She will liberate you from every chain. Let Her hold you. Let Her love you now, today, even if you fall over and over again. God finds us in our guilt, cleanses us of shame, and raises us to victory. God made us free to love. We are not perfect, but we are Hers. We are all in this together.

If you want to change some aspect of your life, invite God into your plans. Commit to the changes you want to make. Envision your life as you wish it to be. Write, paint, sing, talk, or pray about the person you want to be, what matters to you most, and how you want to live your life.

Let go of bitterness and resentment. Open the hurting parts of yourself to God and trusted people who share in your pain. You do not need to carry anything alone. Find ways to heal rather than hiding from whatever hurts. Talk about it. Let the hurt open your heart to compassion for others. Let the suffering move you to do something good that you would not have otherwise done. Turn away from idols and seek the path to lasting and authentic joy. As is written in 1 John 5: 3-4, "For the love of God is this, that we keep his commandments. And his commandments are not burdensome, for whoever is begotten by God conquers the world. And the victory that conquers the world is our faith."

Freedom can be challenging, but we were made to be free. Be well, my friend. Live in the light of God's saving love.

Love,

Aaron

FOR THE DAY YOU ADMIT TO YOURSELF THAT YOU HAVE A PROBLEM WITH ALCOHOL OR DRUGS

"So whoever is in Christ is a new creation: the old things have passed away; behold, new things have come."

- 2 Corinthians 5: 17

Dear Brother, Dear Sister, Dear Friend,

Suffering is an inescapable aspect of our human condition, and there are moments when every fiber of our being screams for relief. At such times, it can be tempting to turn to substances. Alcohol and drugs numb us to pain, for a while, and they give us a jolt of the feelings we desire, such as well-being, relaxation, ecstasy, or satisfaction. Sometimes we look around and perceive that those who drink or use drugs seem happy, and we want to be like them. We want to belong with them.

But the emotions and senses created by alcohol and drugs are not real. These deceptive chemicals play in our brains and wreak havoc. Substances trigger a rush or calm things down in the short-term, but when the high wears off, we are left with the same problems, the same struggles, and the same life. Beer, booze, and drugs keep us from facing reality and prohibit us from building the skills

192

or relationships we need to learn, heal, grow, and ultimately triumph.

As I studied social work at the University of Washington, one of my wisest professors, Wendy Lustbader, taught that substances create a wall between people and the emotions or experiences they do not want to face, such as guilt, shame, grief, anger, fear, self-pity, insecurity, doubt, and trauma. When people use substances to avoid pain, they never learn to cope in healthy ways. They never grow and never learn to conquer their demons. Instead, addiction brings with it a new set of problems that are avoided with continued use of drugs or alcohol.

Growing up gay often yields pain we wish desperately to escape. Some of us face the rejection of family or friends, the fear of judgement, or the loneliness of solitude. Many of us experience confusion as we try to figure out who we really are or where we belong. The world does not make it easy when it splits into opposite extremes. One camp tells us to be celibate forever and one camp tells us to do whatever we want without any sense of obligation to a higher power. And then each of us face unique experiences of pain and hardship. Our hearts break, loved ones die, we survive abuse, or dreams shatter. It becomes more and more tempting to hide all this hurt behind a chemical wall and never think about it.

Drug and alcohol use has consequences. People who use substances often end up bringing great pain upon themselves and their loved ones. Unfortunately, we live in a world that encourages us to ignore or minimize the effects of drinking and drugs. It takes some people years to realize the damaging effects of substances on their lives.

I am proud of you for having the courage to read this letter. Something has opened your eyes and you see that you have a problem. Things need to change. Maybe you were graced with an insight from God, or maybe something painful happened and forced you to face reality. Maybe you hurt someone physically or emotionally because you lost control of your actions when you were drunk or high. Or maybe someone hurt you. Maybe you lost a job or your performance in school suffered because substances kept you from following through on your commitments. Maybe you put yourself or others at risk of sexually transmitted infections because you were too impacted by drugs or alcohol to make safer choices. Maybe you are finding it hard to truly connect with others, show them who you are, and get to know other people deeply because your social life is built around chemically-induced feelings rather than intimacy, communication, and trust. Maybe you feel like your brain is deteriorating, your thoughts are numbing, and you are losing the ability to enjoy anything other than the next buzz or high.

You deserve better than this. No one deserves to be hurt, not you and not anyone else. Regardless of where you have been or what you have done, you deserve to be cherished and loved in authentic relationships with people who care about the real you. Knowing this stems from faith in God's unconditional love for us. In Ephesians 3: 17-19, St. Paul writes, "...that Christ may dwell in your hearts through faith; that you, rooted and grounded in love, may have strength to comprehend with all the holy ones what is the breadth and length and height and depth, and to know the love of Christ that surpasses knowledge, so that you may be filled with the fullness of God." You deserve a life that is rich with adventure, learning, and meaning. When we play dangerous games with our brains and hide from life, we block out God. We refuse to allow God to hold us in the pain, heal us, and lift us to joyful heights beyond anything found in a needle, pill, or bottle. I am not telling you to hate yourself and dwell forever in guilt and shame. Rather, I am inviting you to accept the grace of Jesus so that you can live a new life starting today.

There are various levels of addiction, but drugs and alcohol always have power to hurt us. It takes courage to acknowledge you have a problem and make the decision to work toward change. Here you are today, ready to face something that has spiraled out of control. Where should you go from here?

As with any challenge in life, begin with prayer. Problems with addiction are beyond our capacity to solve on our own. We need God's loving grace to carry us through recovery. Give God your struggles and your pain.

Open your heart to Him and let Him guide you on your journey. Through each step, each failure, and each victory, keep talking to God. Even if you cannot feel God's presence or see His impact on your life, trust that He is there. God is always walking beside you, lifting you up, and giving you what you need when you need it. He is a fountain of strength, courage, wisdom, determination, peace, and grace. God is here to see you through this. Trust Him. As is written in Isaiah 41: 10, "Fear not, I am with you; be not dismayed; I am your God. I will strengthen you, and help you, and uphold you with my right hand of justice."

In addition to seeking God's help, it is absolutely vital to reach out to good people who will support you in recovery. To stop using, we need help as we change all habits related to drugs and alcohol. It is arrogant and foolish to think we can stay clean sober on our own. We might be able to cut off use of drugs and alcohol for a little while, but we need to work with others and with God to experience deeper healing and transformation. If we fail to change on a deeper level, the root issues that led to our substance abuse will never go away. In time, we will likely relapse or fall into new self-destructive or hurtful behaviors in another area of life.

Why is working with other people so important to recovery? We need people outside ourselves to help us understand why we were using, how to heal from the pain of the past, how to make amends for the harm we have done, how to make meaning of our lives moving forward, and how to avoid the people, places, situations, and events that make us want to use.

Start by talking to trusted people in your life who value sobriety. Tell them about your struggles and ask for their support. Many find valuable community in groups like Alcoholics Anonymous or Narcotics Anonymous. If you tried one of these groups and did not like it, try another one. Each group has its own culture, its own approach, and its own style. Keep looking until you find the right group for you. Some people also work with a one-on-one chemical dependency counselor. These professionals are trained to walk the journey with you, help you figure out why you were using in the first place, and help you make a plan for how to build a new, healthier, happier life. Some people find support through programs rooted in important cultural experiences, such as American Indian drum circles or Bible study groups focused on recovery. Some people spend time in a residential rehab program so they can focus on recovery twenty-four hours a day and feel like they are truly starting over. To connect with treatment services near you, call the Substance Abuse and Mental Health Administration National Helpline at 1-800-662-4357.

Think, pray, and talk to trusted loved ones about what kinds of treatment and support might work best for you. Lean on mentors, teachers, coaches, pastors, family members, and friends who are committed to sharing unconditional love with you and supporting you in being clean and sober. As you go through this journey, you may realize there are people who do not support you. Some people may actively want you to keep using, and others may say they support you but their continued drug or alcohol use tempts you to relapse. These are not necessarily bad people. They could be people you love very much who love you back. But at this time, the way to love them best may be to tell them honestly that you cannot see them until they commit to making changes in their own lives. If you really want to live a clean and sober life, you need to make hard choices. You can pray for them. You can care about them. You can hope that they will change in the future. But until you have compelling evidence that they will not tempt you to relapse, you need to let them go. You cannot help them if they do not want to be helped, and you cannot help anyone if you are pulled again and again into substance abuse.

As you walk through the journey of recovery, ask God for a vision of a new and better life. What is God's dream for you? Who did He create you to be? God does not intend for us to hide from reality or seek shadows of peace in bottles, needles, powders, pills, or puffs of smoke. We are made to be Temples of the Holy Spirit. We are made to be the Body of Christ alive in the world today. God made you to love and to be loved. God wants us to work with Him, to struggle with Him, to build His Kingdom on earth, to bear the suffering that comes with witnessing to the truth and advocating for justice. He brings us to Him so that we may rise with Christ.

We will suffer and we will make mistakes. When we face the pain and refuse to hide from it, we share in the redemptive suffering of Christ. Our hurt and our very selves must be transformed by Jesus, not avoided through drugs and alcohol. As it says in 2 Corinthians 5: 17, "So whoever is in Christ is a new creation: the old things have passed away; behold, new things have come."

So please, as soon as you put down this letter, seek help. You are loved dearly by God. Trust that He will give you the strength to overcome any addiction and any source of pain in your life. When it seems like there is no way out, remember the words of Mark 10: 27: "Jesus looked at them and said, 'For human beings it is impossible, but not for God. All things are possible for God." Remind yourself over and over again the words of Philippians 4: 13: "I have the strength for everything through him who empowers me." Face your demons with God by your side so that you may build character, grow in faith, discover true joy, and draw others to God.

Love,

Aaron

FOR WHEN YOU LOSE SOMEONE YOU LOVE

"Jesus said to her, 'Your brother will rise.' Martha said to him, 'I know he will rise, in the resurrection on the last day.' Jesus told her, 'I am the resurrection and the life; whoever believes in me, even if he dies, will live, and everyone who lives and believes in me will never die. Do you believe this?' She said to him, 'Yes, Lord. I have come to believe that you are the Messiah, the Son of God, the one who is coming into the world.'"

- John 11: 23-27

Dear Sister, Dear Brother, Dear Friend,

I am so sorry for your loss. Grief is one of the great burdens of life. There is no way to prepare for it. Sometimes we lose someone suddenly through an accident, act of violence, or health emergency. Sometimes we watch a loved one suffer and die slowly through serious illness. Regardless of how it happens, the harsh reality of death changes everything. The pain of it cannot be fixed or chased away. It hurts, or it leaves a terrifying emptiness. When we lose someone to death, there remains in our hearts a yearning ache to speak with the person who is missing, to complete the business that was left undone, to ask for forgiveness, to offer mercy, to say I love you, to have one more moment being together and breathing the same air. We want things that seem impossible. The beloved seems to be gone in a way that feels overwhelmingly final.

As Christians, we believe in resurrection, yet death remains a great mystery. We cling to hope that passing away is not the end, that death is the door that unites us with God, and that we will be raised again by God through Christ. This faith is our only hope. We must trust in things we cannot see and cannot understand. But even if we believe in life after death, we still find ourselves today at a juncture of devastation and loss. We hold onto the promise of eternal life, but it feels like our little boat is trapped in the heart of the storm. With wind this strong and waves this deep, how can we be expected to walk on water?

Jesus, being fully human, grieved in his own lifetime. The Bible tells us that "Jesus wept" when he stood outside the tomb of his friend, Lazarus (John 11: 35). His conversation with Lazarus' sister, Martha, stands across time as a powerful witness to the hope that we have through Jesus: "Jesus said to her, 'Your brother will rise.' Martha said to him, 'I know he will rise, in the resurrection on the last day.' Jesus told her, 'I am the resurrection and the life; whoever believes in me, even if he dies, will live, and everyone who lives and believes in me will never die. Do you believe this?' She said to him, 'Yes, Lord. I have come to believe that you are the Messiah, the Son of God, the one who is coming into the world'" (John 11: 23-27). With Martha, all we can do is place our hope in Christ.

Yet even the disciples who met Jesus face to face struggled with fear, doubt, and heartbreak. Listen to how some of the disciples grieved after the death of Jesus in Luke 27: 59-61: "Taking the body, Joseph wrapped it in clean linen and laid it in his new tomb that he had hewn in the rock. Then he rolled a huge stone across the entrance to the tomb and departed. But Mary Magdalene and the other Mary remained sitting there, facing the tomb." The truth is once the work of honoring the dead through burial is done, all we can do is sit and face the tomb. We need to abide with our grief and face it. Our only hope is to wait on God for the promised resurrection.

What is it like for you to sit with grief? The loss of a loved one sometimes leaves us feeling empty or depleted. There are times when it feels like nothing around us is real, or like everything around us keeps moving while we remain frozen and numb. Sometimes we are overcome by rage and the unfairness of life and death, or deeply depressed and unable to imagine any happiness in a life without the person we lost. Sometimes we feel guilty when we think about the possibility of being happy again. We wonder what kind of person could be happy in a world where their mother, father, lover, friend, or other loved one is gone. We may also feel intense guilt for something we feel we did or did not do while the person was alive.

Grief becomes complicated and confusing when there was conflict or tension between the survivor and the deceased. As gay Christians, we are not strangers with conflict and tension. Perhaps you felt rejected by the person you lost, or perhaps they passed away before you were able to fully trust them, open up to them, or share with them some essential truth about who you are. Perhaps forgiveness was never offered or received.

What should we to do with emptiness, anger, sorrow, unfinished business, guilt, and despair? We must begin by being honest with ourselves and turning everything over to God. There is a great temptation to run away from our thoughts and emotions, to drown everything in drugs, alcohol, sex, or too much work. These unhealthy behaviors will only bring more problems, and the grief will still be there when the high wears off. It is important to practice healthy coping skills at this difficult time. Exercise, go for walks, pray, talk to loved ones, write, sketch, paint, read, and stay engaged in everyday life activities like school or work.

However, also give yourself time to face what has happened. Give God your struggles and your doubts. Ask Her to guide you on your journey of healing. If you are angry with God, pray about it. God can handle your anger. If you find it hard to believe in God, pray about it. God can handle your doubt. If you have no idea where to go from here, pray about it. God can handle your confusion. If you want to give up, pray about it. God can handle your despair. God will always meet you where you are if you let Her.

Whatever you are going through, give it to God, talk about it, and open your heart to transformation, growth, and healing. Talk with trusted loved ones as well, for God works through the people in our lives and God works through us. We are called to be the hands and feet of Christ for each other.

Everyone grieves in their own way. As long as you avoid hurting yourself and others, let yourself be sad when you need to be sad, angry when you need to be angry, and confused when you need to be confused. Let the emotions be storms that come and go, and try to remember that no storm lasts forever.

In your grief, remember and honor the person you lost. Meditate on who they were, the good and the bad. Share stories with others who loved them. Write down your memories. Look at pictures. Thank God for everything they taught you, the happy times you had together, and the ways this person helped you become the person you are today. Pray for them. Ask God to hold them with a tender love that never dies.

When you are ready, talk to the person you lost. Visit their grave, write them a letter, or speak to their spirit directly from your heart. Ask for the apology you deserve or offer the apology you need to give. Tell them the secret you want them to know. Ask the question you wish you had asked when you last saw them, face to face. Listen to whatever message comes to your heart. If you hear nothing, then sit in the silence with God, and try to believe that your answer will arrive with time.

As Christians, we have faith that we are made in the image and likeness of God. We are made for eternal life. Death does not end life, but death changes it. Death does not end our relationships, but death changes them. I hope and pray that as you move through your journey of grief, you eventually come to trust that your loved one is at peace with God. We must have hope that in the fullness of time, death will be no more. As is written in 1 Corinthians 15: 26, "The last enemy to be destroyed is death." With hope in the resurrection given to us through Christ, we can say with St. Paul, "Where, O death, is your victory? Where, O death, is your sting?" (1 Corinthians 15: 55).

And yet, sometimes we must weep, because while death does not hold eternal victory, it still hurts us today. This pain of separation and change is temporary, but it remains deep and unfathomable. What can we do? As Jesus carried his cross on the day of his crucifixion, Luke 23: 27-28 tells us, "A large crowd of people followed Jesus, including many women who mourned and lamented him. Jesus turned to them and said, 'Daughters of Jerusalem, do not weep for me; weep instead for yourselves and for your children…'" These tender and poignant words of our Lord affirm that while we remain alive on earth, it is right to weep and mourn at times of loss. Jesus's incarnation and resurrection shattered the veil that separated human beings from God, and we meet God throughout the moments of daily life. Yet the fullness of the Kingdom of God has not yet come to be. We still build it together with God, day by day. And so there are times when the pain of sin and death cut deep. And so we weep, because we know deep down this is not the way things are meant to be.

This moment of Jesus's passion also teaches us that while we carry our own grief, we must also open our hearts to encounter others who are hurting. As he suffered, Jesus told others to weep not for him, but for themselves. He saw their anguish and he ministered to them, even at the moment of his own great agony.

Like Jesus, we are also called to minster to others while we suffer. We cannot let ourselves be so lost in grief that we abandon our duty to love God, love our neighbors, and love ourselves. We are not the only ones who lost a loved one, and so there are others who need our love and support. When people hurt together, they are sometimes tempted to push people away. Therefore, we might feel inclined to say or do cruel things to those around us to keep them at a distance.

But we can overcome these urges. We do not need to hurt others in our grief. We can choose to open up to one another, care for one another, support each other, and carry each other through this hardship. We all make mistakes. We need to give each other grace, especially during times of emotional turmoil. Maybe you have lashed out in anger at others, or maybe others are pulling away from you and shutting you out. We cannot tell others how to grieve, and sometimes their actions will hurt us. You might need a parent, sibling, or friend who is letting you down. Pray for them. Try to see their actions as tragic results of grief that have nothing to do with how much they love you. If you think it would help to talk to them, then give it a try. Set healthy boundaries and take space from people if they are saying or doing anything that hurts you. All the while, pray that you may follow in the footsteps of Jesus and minister to others in their grief as he ministers to us from the cross.

Once again, it can be tempting to try and escape pain or emptiness through any means available, even if the method is destructive to ourselves or hurtful to others. We may want to numb ourselves to pain or shake ourselves from the fog of apathy with drugs, alcohol, or loveless sex. We may choose to rail against the unfairness of death by fighting, bickering, or seeking to control other people. We may engage in self-harm or fantasize about escape through suicide. If you find yourself coping in these or other unhealthy ways, please seek help right away. Talk to a family member or close friend. Talk to a trusted teacher, pastor, or mentor. Connect with a counselor, or if you are seriously thinking about ending your own life, go to a nearby hospital. You are precious and the world needs you.

God will take you home when the time is right, but there is a lot of life for you to live until that day comes.

It is hard for me to write about the moments of my grief, but I do so in order to show the healing power of God's love in my life. My sister, Kerry, carried baby Henry for just over 20 weeks. He was not born yet, but we all loved him fiercely. He was my parents' first grandchild. Kerry and her husband, Jared, had so many dreams for the life their son would lead. They would read him stories, teach him to play football, and have him baptized in the church where they got married. He was my little nephew, and I was planning to go part-time at work so that I could help take care of him two days a week.

I got the phone call late one afternoon a couple days before Christmas. Kerry called me from her doctor's office and said they could not find Henry's heartbeat. I met her at the hospital and we wept together as the midwife confirmed that Kerry's baby boy had died. There was nothing poetic or romantic about the pain that followed. Henry was dead. He never got the chance to take his first breath, lie in his mother's arms, play with his father's beard, or bounce on his uncle's knee. He would never grow up and be the man he was meant to be. His death was harsh, sudden, and cruel. It was not right. It reminded us of so many other unfair deaths that have touched my family- my mother's two miscarriages, a child my mother tutored in our home who was killed by a drunk driver, the daughter of one of my beloved teachers who died of cancer, a family friend who died of a gunshot wound, a classmate who was killed by an infection from a feeding tube that was placed after a tragic accident, a preschool student who died of sudden illness, a co-worker who died of cancer two years after getting married while she was trying to conceive a child.

We did what we could to support Kerry and Jared. They were strong through their grief, but there were so many questions for us to face. Why did this happen? Why do bad things happen to good people? Why do bad things happen at all? Where is Henry now? Can he hear us when we talk to him? How do we make it through this tragedy, and why should we keep going?

The only thing that kept me alive through it all was the love of God. I do not know why God allows bad things to happen, but I firmly believe that She holds and heals us when they do. My only hope is that Henry lives on with God. I like to think that Jesus and Mary care for him as he plays with the babies my mother lost. I like to think they will watch over us until the time comes when we are all reunited.

It is important for me to remember that Henry's life on earth had meaning. He brought joy to his entire family every day he bounced around my sister's womb. I will never forget him and I will never stop loving him. I know the same is true for Kerry, Jared, and the rest of my family. Losing Henry hurts, but I am thankful I had the chance to know and love him while he was here.

And so, through your grief, cling to God. Offer all you think, feel, and do to the one who created us and gives us everlasting life. Even when it seems impossible, believe that your loved one remains safe in the hands of the Creator. Remember the words of Revelation 21: 3-4: "I heard a loud voice from the throne saying, 'Behold, God's dwelling is with the human race. He will dwell with them and they will be his people and God himself will always be with them as their God. He will wipe every tear from their eyes, and there shall be no more death or mourning, wailing or pain, for the old order has passed away.'"

We need to carry each other through grief, and we need God to carry us through life. Ultimately, we must remember that the reason death is so painful is that life is good. The reason loss is so painful is because love is good. I am deeply moved by the following poem, written by Ellen Bass (2002):

<u>The Thing Is</u>
to love life, to love it even
when you have no stomach for it
and everything you've held dear
crumbles like burnt paper in your hands,
your throat filled with the silt of it.
When grief sits with you, its tropical heat

210

thickening the air, heavy as water
more fit for gills than lungs;
when grief weights you like your own flesh
only more of it, an obesity of grief,
you think, *How can a body withstand this?*
Then you hold life like a face
Between your palms, a plain face,
no charming smile, no violet eyes,
and you say, yes, I will take you
I will love you, again. (p. 72)

We must choose to love life, for loving life is indeed a choice. It is easy to succumb to doubt and despair. It is easy to give up. But even when we feel hopeless, we must open our eyes and search for goodness in the world. There is love to heal every shattered heart, and there is life beyond the grave. As we read in Psalm 118: 24, "This is the day the LORD has made; let us rejoice in it and be glad." Try even in the midst of grief to embrace the day. Cling to your loved ones and believe that God will wipe every tear from your eyes. Someday, death will be no more. Hang in there.

Love,

Aaron

FOR THE DAY YOU ARE READY TO LET GO OF YOUR MISERY

"Yet it was our infirmities that he bore, our sufferings that he endured, while we thought of him as stricken, as one smited by God and afflicted. But he was pierced for our offenses, crushed for our sins, upon him was the chastisement that makes us whole, by his stripes we were healed."

- Isaiah 53: 4-5

Dear Brother, Dear Sister, Dear Friend,

Most of us do not really want to hurt. As human beings, we are born with instincts that direct us to seek pleasure and avoid pain. This is a fact of life. Yet people are complicated. Sometimes we get used to suffering and it becomes difficult to imagine life without it. We all have different stories about the sources of our pain. Some of us survive trauma, bullying, or abuse. Some of us internalize low self-esteem after years of subtle negative messages and overt emotional attacks. Sometimes we are so overwhelmed by guilt and shame that we blame ourselves for everything wrong with the world. Whatever the cause, pain sometimes eats at our hearts and kills our joy. It is exhausting, and yet familiar. Some of us do not know what life would be like without it. If we are honest, the thought of truly healing and leaving all the hurt behind can be frightening.

212

Yet Jesus did not suffer, die, and rise again for us to persist in our misery. He came to set us free. Luke's gospel tells us that Jesus goes to his home town of Nazareth, reads the following passage from Isaiah, and later states that these words are fulfilled through him: "The Spirit of the Lord is upon me, because he has anointed me to bring glad tidings to the poor. He has sent me to proclaim liberty to captives and recovery of sight to the blind, to let the oppressed go free, and to proclaim a year acceptable to the Lord" (Luke 4: 18-19). If Jesus came to heal our spirits and free us from evil and sin, why are the burdens of sorrow and guilt so difficult to escape?

Sometimes we find ourselves trapped in abusive situations. Suffering continues because we have not yet escaped the root experiences that cause it. Maybe you depend on a parent or romantic partner for shelter and all the basic necessities of life. If that person hurts you, you might stay because you feel like you have nowhere else to go. Or perhaps you feel paralyzed by violence, threats, fear, and manipulation. Maybe somebody in your life does everything they can to control what you think, feel, and do. Despair seeps in whenever we cannot find a road to freedom or hope.

If this is your situation, know that God is with you. He is by your side, suffers with you, and wants you to find liberty and peace. Pray for the wisdom to know all your options, and pray for the support you need to survive and thrive. Open your heart and let God guide you through this. When you are ready, there are resources in place to help. Whether you want to escape or remain living where you are, you can reach out to counselors, advocates, support groups, faith-based social service programs, youth groups, shelters, legal supports, crisis lines, child abuse lines, and helpful people who have been through similar situations. If you feel ready to connect with support of any kind, call the National Domestic Violence Hotline at 1-800-799-7233. The person who answers will help you find the resources you need and make a plan to stay safe.

Whenever you choose to make a change or act, it is important to be safe and thoughtful. It is always dangerous to leave an abuser. You need to make sure you have a solid place to land and people around who can help protect you. Only you know what you need most. To begin building your plan, talk it over with God in prayer, then reach out to trusted people and competent professionals who can help you stay safe. I hope and pray you find your way to a better situation soon.

Sometimes we escape painful situations but the after-effects will not go away. We still believe the hateful words someone said to us years ago. We still think the person we see in the mirror is ugly and worthless. We still feel depressed, miserable, anxious, or hopeless. Sometimes we might even wish we were dead or think the world would be better off without us. In other words, it still hurts. And the shocking truth is that sometimes we do not really want to feel better. Sometimes we cling to the sorrow, emptiness, despair, and shame. We refuse to let it go.

There are many reasons why we hold onto our pain. For some of us, it is all we know. Change can be terrifying, especially when changes in the past have been chaotic, unexpected, or hurtful. Sometimes we come to resist change because we have learned to be afraid of it.

Other times we do not let ourselves even *want* to feel better because we are afraid of being disappointed. We think, *Why should I try to feel happy when I will probably fail and then feel worse than I already do?* It seems easier to persist and survive that it does to expend energy and effort in what feels like a lost cause.

Furthermore, if we are honest, sometimes there is a morbid satisfaction in being unhappy, dwelling in self-pity, and forever licking our emotional wounds. It does not feel good, but on some level it makes us feel alive. The pain of the past becomes a little less horrible if we focus on the rush of today's heartbreak or crisis. It is an emotional form of self-harm, and like actual physical self-harm, it is a coping skill that leaves behind its own damage.

Another reason we cling to pain is that it sometimes becomes the glue that holds together our relationships with friends or dating partners. Bonds formed over stories of brokenness and suffering can be powerful, but they quickly become unhealthy if they are not balanced with mutual support and honest joy.

And, of course, many of us remain miserable because we think we do not deserve to be happy. Deep down, we believe our suffering is a result of our own sins and failures. We punish ourselves as if justice demands it.

Change might make things worse, but it can also make things better. We often need to give up an old way of life before experiencing something new. As Jesus says in John 12: 24, "Amen, amen, I say to you, unless a grain of wheat falls to the ground and dies, it remains just a grain of wheat; but if it dies, it produces much fruit." At some point, we need to take a leap of faith and use our reason, our resources, our healthy relationships, and our trust in God's guidance to leave the past behind and move forward.

If fear of disappointment holds us back from trying to be happy, then despair wins before we even try to make things better. We may not be able to make all our problems go away overnight, but we can take one step at a time, search for signs of progress, and celebrate each small victory. God's grace will heal us in time.

Hope prevails when we continue believing in the saving power of God and keep moving forward. We feel most alive when we love God, serve our neighbors, and bring other people joy. It is hard to love and serve when we are miserable. Furthermore, relationships built on selfless love, kindness, generosity, and trust are healthier than those built on a mutual hatred for life. Of course, we need to be authentic. As we build trust, it is good to share experiences of vulnerability and pain. But the purpose of sharing must be to bring each other healing, not to dwell together in endless, hopeless misery. Love demands that we work for the other's good, for the other's joy, for the other's healing. 1 Corinthians 8: 1 teaches us that, "… love builds up." If we truly love one another, we must help build each other up into the people God made us to be.

When we feel we do not deserve to be happy, we must remember that God's unconditional mercy rests at the heart of the Christian message. Jesus did not save us from sin because we earned it. Jesus saved us because God wants us to be in joyful relationship with Him regardless of the past. As St. Paul writes in Romans 8: 1-2, "Hence, now there is no condemnation for those who are in Christ Jesus. For the law of the spirit of life in Christ Jesus has freed you from the law of sin and death."

I cannot convince you to desire joy. I cannot make you want anything, and I should not even try. You need to live your life and walk your emotional journey with God. For the sake of your own happiness and well-being, I hope you come to a place where you are ready to give God your pain and let it go. Are you there? Are you ready to begin healing? I hope so. The sacrifice of Jesus was great, and it was made in love so that we may enjoy life and love one another.

So please, I beg you, pray. Invite the Holy Spirit to come upon you and refresh your soul. Ask God to heal your wounds and work through them to deepen compassion for yourself and others. Reflect on the words of Jeremiah 17: 14, "Heal me, LORD, that I may be healed; save me, that I may be saved, for it is you whom I praise."

The journey through healing is different for everyone, but God always walks with us as we make our way. As I studied social work in graduate school, one of my professors, Wendy Lustbader, explained that one key element of healing is telling one's story of pain or trauma in the presence of a caring other. You can begin by telling your story to God. Pray. Journal. Talk to your Creator about the things you have been through and the things that hurt. God wants to listen. When you are ready, find a person to talk to, whether they be a friend, family member, pastor, or therapist. Find someone you trust who wants to listen and wants to help you heal.

Professor Lustbader also taught us the importance of ultimately moving toward a place of compassion and understanding for those who hurt us. This often seems unfathomable and impossible, yet it is a clear calling of our faith as Christians. Jesus says in Matthew 5: 44-45, "But I say to you, love your enemies, and pray for those who persecute you, that you may be children of your heavenly Father, for he makes his sun rise on the bad and the good, and causes rain to fall on the just and the unjust." Jesus is not asking us to ignore, rationalize, or accept abuse. Rather, he is asking us to see our enemies as human beings loved by God, hope for their redemption, and pray for peace. When we understand the stories of our enemies, our eyes open to their brokenness and miracles happen in our own hearts. We realize, perhaps for the first time, that what happened to us is not our fault. The people who hurt us were broken by sin long before we came along, and we have power through Christ to replace the bitterness in our hearts with mercy. Step by step, day by day, we can let go of the past and begin again.

As we move through healing, we often realize that histories of pain deepen our compassion and move us to active roles of loving service. Meanwhile, we must celebrate that we survived, enjoy life, and thank God for each new day. When we decide to be happier, everything changes. In my early twenties, I convinced myself I had to be celibate because I was gay. When I opened myself up to the idea of dating, I was convinced no one would ever want me. I remained hyper-functional during this season of life and excelled in school and work, but on the inside I was an emotional mess. I took long walks around my hometown and thought over and over again about how lonely I was. I was convinced nothing would ever change. I made family and friends miserable by talking endlessly about how I never felt like I belonged anywhere and that I did not know what I was doing with my life. I felt ugly and worthless.

People would say wonderful things that would cheer me up for a moment, and then I'd fall back into the same old slump. It may sound pathetic, but there were many days when I woke up, dragged myself out of bed, stared myself down in the bathroom mirror, and said out loud, "A few more decades of this and then you get to die."

And the sad truth is that, miserable as I was, part of me kind of liked feeling this way. There is something romantic about crying alone while listening to depressing music at maximum volume. And through all this period, I felt close to God because He always met me in the pain. I meditated on Scriptures about dying with Christ so that I might rise with him. I felt like God was the only one who understood me and like I was achieving great spiritual depth and maturity. I now realize that I was less like a wise old sage and more like a sobbing child being comforted by a loving parent. I did grow closer to God through this struggle, but God never wanted me to sit around moping and wanting to die. God made me to love and serve with the joy of the Holy Spirit alive in my heart. God held me close in those difficult days because I was broken and hurting. But as I healed, I came to realize that God holds me just as close in moments of peace and joy. Love remains through times of hardship and times of prosperity. That is why sorrow and defeat never have the final say no matter what our circumstances may be. We can always abide in the love of God, no matter what. We are made to love God, love our neighbors, and love ourselves, and we are called to do these things at all times, no matter how we feel.

One of the key milestones in my journey took place when I realized I could do a lot more good when I am healthy, happy, and filled with God's peace. I do not need to be fake-happy all the time or sugary-sweet in all my interactions with others. I need to be authentic and let people know I have ups and downs. To pretend otherwise would be a lie, and God wants us to tell the truth. But through the hills and valleys of life, I need to open my heart to the healing love of God. I want to do God's will in my life, and it is hard to hear God's voice when my mind is filled with the banging clamor of misery and self-doubt. Emotions are contagious, and I would rather make other people happy than sad.

And so, today, open yourself to the Holy Spirit of God. As is written in Psalm 95: 7, "For this is our God whose people we are, God's well-tended flock. Oh, that today you would hear his voice." Let God speak to you, fill you, heal you, and love you. Believe that God can bring you joy, because He can. As Christians, we believe that the words of Isaiah 53: 4-5 prophesy about the healing power of Christ: "Yet it was our infirmities that he bore, our sufferings that he endured, while we thought of him as stricken, as one smited by God and afflicted. But he was pierced for our offenses, crushed for our sins, upon him was the chastisement that makes us whole, by his stripes we were healed." Accepting God's healing is not always easy. We need to tear down walls and defenses to give God access to our wounds, and we might feel worse for a short time before we feel better. But if you are ready, the journey is worth it. God will give you peace and transform you into the person the world needs you to be.

Love,

Aaron

PART FIVE: LETTERS OF INSPIRATION: Follow God and embrace the mission that has been set before you.

FOR THE DAY YOU REALIZE YOU HAVE NO IDEA WHAT YOU WANT TO DO WITH YOUR LIFE

"Make known to me your ways, LORD; teach me your paths. Guide me in your truth and teach me, for you are God my savior. For you I wait all the long day, because of your goodness, LORD."

\- Psalm 25: 4-5

Dear Sister, Dear Brother, Dear Friend,

Does life feel like an adventure full of opportunities to explore new places, meet fascinating people, and do meaningful work? Do you feel a profound sense of peace, like you are doing exactly what you were made to do? Or do you usually feel lost, unsure of who you really are, and unaware of where your true home might be? Sometimes there are tasks placed before us that cannot be denied without great personal cost. We are expected to study hard in school, or care for a sick relative, or work evenings in the family restaurant. Duty often comes with the clarity and grace needed to accomplish it, though we are always free to turn our backs if we choose to do so.

Yet other times the way is not so clear. We might feel trapped in a life we did not ask for and no longer want, or we might find ourselves at a crossroads and have no idea where to turn next. Maybe we struggle to discern what we should study in school, where we should live, what career we should pursue, who to date, or how to spend our days. Sometimes we have clear dreams of what we want, but we cannot see how to overcome economic hardship, previous responsibilities, and oppressive social barriers.

It can be difficult to discover who we are, find our way, and build a life around our passions. As gay Christians, we are sometimes forced to expend a great deal of time and energy discovering or hiding our identities, justifying our choices, and searching for places to belong. This takes away from exploring, practicing, and living out the other important aspects of our lives. Our sexualities and gender identities are vital and beautiful parts of ourselves that deeply impact how we relate to others. Yet we are more than sexual beings. Each of us is endowed by our Creator with unique personalities, talents, strengths, gifts, insights, and passions. Life is an opportunity to share everything we are with others through love. We need to celebrate our sexual identities while also discovering and living out the other passions and dreams that make us full human beings.

If you are struggling with where to go on your journey, pray the words of Psalm 25: 4-5: "Make known to me your ways, LORD; teach me your paths. Guide me in your truth and teach me, for you are God my savior. For you I wait all the long day, because of your goodness, LORD." God is with us each step of the way as we move through life. If we trust in God, She will move our hearts and lead us to relationships with good, caring people who can help us make sense of life.

Through it all, we must remain faithful to the great commandments. We read in Mark 12: 28-31: "One of the scribes, when he came forward and heard them disputing and saw how well he had answered them, asked him, 'Which is the first of all the commandments?' Jesus replied, 'The first is this: 'Hear, O Israel! The Lord our God is Lord alone! You shall love the Lord your God with all your heart, with all your soul, with all your mind, and with all your strength.' The second is this: 'You shall love your neighbor as yourself.' There is no other commandment greater than these.'" Jesus gives us clear guideposts for making the deep decisions of our lives. In all our pursuits, we must reflect on the following questions in prayer and conversation with others: *Does this path lead me to love God with all my heart, soul, mind, and strength? Does this path lead me to love my neighbor? Does this path lead me to love myself?*

When we think about what to do with our time on earth, we must look beyond how we earn a living. Ultimately, we are called to live as loving disciples of Jesus Christ. Thankfully, this can and must be done at all times through everything we are and everything we do.

There is more to life than finding the ideal job. Selfless love, passion, and faith should fill our lives and drive all of our pursuits. Maybe we will be paid for doing something we absolutely love, or maybe we will work hard at a job we tolerate so that we can take care of ourselves and our families. We are not failures as long as we offer our efforts to God and hope that whatever we do somehow contributes to the greater good. After the work day is done, many of us will build energy and meaning through loving relationships, creative projects, volunteer service, educational pursuits, and spiritual endeavors. One can be a restaurant worker by day and an actor by night. One might work as an engineer while also volunteering as an art teacher at a local community center. One can work as a construction worker while taking night classes in theology and ministry. Living a full life must include meeting our practical obligations while also making time for the special interests and dreams God plants in our hearts. Everything must be balanced with the universal call to love God, love our neighbors, and love ourselves.

Sometimes we are led to think that if we find the right job, it will make us feel happy and fulfilled all the time. The reality is that there is good and bad to every job. Work requires effort, compromise, self-sacrifice, and critical thinking. It takes time to build skills and competencies, and we often need to make mistakes so that we can learn from them. Most of us will probably never find a job that makes us happy all the time. In fact, nothing in this world has the power to make us happy all the time. But that's okay. How can we learn and grow if we are always happy? How can we experience compassion for those who suffer if we are always happy? How can we be fully human if our emotional life is a one-noted drone of endless happiness? Constant good-feelings should not be the goal. Rather, we must pursue work that uses our greatest strengths to make positive impacts in our communities and the world.

At the end of the day, all vocations are opportunities to serve if they are lived with hearts that love deeply. Some people provide direct service as teachers, social workers, firefighters, healthcare workers, or political agents. Some people, such as painters, musicians, writers, publishers, and museum operators, create or distribute art through which others learn and grow. Pastors, youth ministers, and church leaders actively spread the word of God and build up the Body of Christ. Merchants, retail workers, and executives have the power to support robust economies, maintain ethical business practices, and equitably share profits so that communities thrive. Farm workers produce the food that sustains human life, and engineers, architects, laborers, construction workers, electricians, plumbers, and other professionals build and operate the infrastructure that makes peaceful societies possible. To find the setting where our efforts will bear the most fruit, we must look at the stories of our lives. Pray about these questions and discuss them with people you trust: *What have I been built for? How can I best serve my community? Will my primary duties be carried out through paid work, volunteer roles, creative pursuits, or personal relationships? How am I called to love where I stand today? Is there another way I am called to love in the future? How can I prepare myself in the here and now?*

Sometimes we put a great deal of pressure on ourselves to find out what we love to do so that we can pursue it professionally. Unfortunately, there are times when nothing special surfaces after deep soul searching, and there are other times when we can think of a thousand things we love to do and it is hard to pick just one. In difficult moments, we are haunted by confusion and do not know where to begin. Perhaps we never had many opportunities to try new things. Perhaps we were limited by lack of resources or time, or we had significant responsibilities that kept us from thinking too much about what we wanted to do when we grew up. Maybe we never felt free to explore anything that met our interests. Or perhaps we were always afraid of failing, of looking foolish, of not being perfect, and so we locked ourselves out of new experiences that may have opened up interesting pathways in our lives.

How do we find our way out of confusion and fear? We must live and listen. If we do not know our own passions yet, we need to get excited about all the discoveries that are yet to be made. If we are overwhelmed by all the many passions we experience, we can delight in diving into them one at a time. Open your eyes to the world around you and decide what you want to try. Take an art class. Look up books at the local library on subjects you want to learn more about. Volunteer for a cause you believe in. Serve food at a soup kitchen, tutor at an after-school program, or march in social justice demonstrations. Interview professionals you admire and ask them why they do what they do. Ask a friend to teach you how to do something they are good at. Sing in your church choir or ask a member of the church band to teach you how to play an instrument. Look up videos that teach you how to do things you want to try, such as sewing, fixing cars, playing guitar, or solving logic problems. Try new things, have fun, and see what sticks.

As you live your life, pay attention to what you are good at and what feels right. Ask people you trust what they perceive to be your greatest strengths. Pray, think, and discuss with others how you can use your strengths in daily life, in relationships, and in your career. If you honestly seek God through love, you will find purpose embedded within every day.

As you go about your journey, avoid the pitfalls of self-centered living, drugs, and alcohol. God wants to help us find our path through life, but if we live only to make ourselves feel good, we will not be able to hear Her voice. As we read in Ephesians 5: 17-20, "Therefore, do not continue in ignorance, but try to understand what is the will of the Lord. And do not get drunk on wine, in which lies debauchery, but be filled with the Spirit, addressing one another in psalms and hymns and spiritual songs, singing and playing always and for everything in the name of our Lord Jesus Christ to God the Father."

Please do not misunderstand me. I am not saying you should never have fun, and I am not saying you should live a somber, joyless lifestyle. Rather, I am asking you to consider that true joy and fulfillment is found in the love of God and fellow human beings. There is wildness and adventure in loving God and loving people. When we live soberly, selflessly, and joyfully, each social interaction becomes a special memory rather than another drunken, blurry night. Each encounter with a fellow journeyer becomes a lesson learned or a taste of God's eternal love.

I hope you find meaning and joy every day. It is not always easy. I spent years wrestling with self-doubt and anxiety over what I should be doing with my life. From the time I was a young child, I have always been deeply moved by the words of Jesus when he describes the final judgement at the end of time. We read in Matthew 25: 34-36: "Then the king will say to those on his right, 'Come, you who are blessed by my Father. Inherit the kingdom prepared for you from the foundation of the world. For I was hungry and you gave me food, I was thirsty and you gave me drink, a stranger and you welcomed me, naked and you clothed me, ill and you cared for me, in prison and you visited me.'" I had received incredible blessings in life and witnessed wonderful examples of service through my father, a state attorney, and my mother, a special education teacher. From gratitude to God and my family, I yearned from the depths of my soul to minister to the needs of others. As I grew up, I saw clearly that there were infinite ways to do this. How could I choose only one?

I felt as if I needed to find the perfect job that allowed me to use all my strengths to make a large, tangible impact on the world. I wanted to feed the hungry and clothe the naked. I wanted to help end modern-day slavery. I wanted to reform labor conditions and increase wages around the world. I wanted to help resolve conflicts, end war, and establish peace everywhere. I realized I had to start somewhere, and so I took on one job at a time. Every job I tried had moments of triumph and moments of defeat. When times grew tough, I assumed the position was a bad fit and I moved on to something else. For example, I taught preschool for several years. There were times when I was overcome with joy as I read to my students, made them laugh, coached them through solving problems, taught positive social skills, and ignited a love for learning. There were other times when I felt exhausted by the intense work load, and I was often discouraged when certain children continued to have emotional and behavioral issues despite my best efforts to help them learn initiative or self-control. I let the negative aspects fuel intense self-doubt until I decided to quit and become a school custodian. In this role, I discovered profound satisfaction in making something clean which was not clean. There were tangible results to my work every day, and the job provided me with creative mental space to daydream and write. Yet I felt lonely in the work. I missed the experience of building positive relationships with others. I went back to school to become a social worker and took a job as a family therapist. I loved listening, teaching positive coping skills, discussing parenting strategies, and offering unconditional support and positive regard. However, I felt overwhelmed with feelings of powerlessness as people came to me with their sorrow, apathy, anger, and brokenness. I put too much pressure on myself to solve other people's problems rather than being a support as they figured things out for themselves. As you can see, I kept moving from role to role in hopes that I would find the perfect job that would meet all of my desires without delivering any sort of struggle or hardship.

It took me years to learn that my search for a perfect job was a false idol that kept me from the truth. We can only find deep meaning and satisfaction when we give every moment in love to God and our neighbors. In the beginning, I wanted to serve God by making some grand impact for social justice. Then I tried to fix the problems of everyone I met. When I let go of my pride and truly surrendered my dreams to God, I realized that She is the savior, not me. My duty is not to save everyone and stop evil, but rather to love unconditionally and allow God to work through me wherever I am.

With this insight, I was able to look at my work history with new eyes. Instead of seeing failure after failure, I saw a narrative of God's grace. God used me to help my preschool students learn a bit about academics and a lot about how to make friends and how to enjoy school. God used me as a custodian to keep schools safe and clean so that students could learn and grow in healthy environments. God used me as a therapist to help young people and their families heal from trauma, meditate on life goals, and build loving relationships with each other. I did not achieve the grand results I hoped for, but through the grace of God, I planted some small seeds of goodness in the lives of others. There is a part of Matthew's gospel where some of Jesus's disciples are unable to exorcise a demon from a little boy. Jesus comes and heals the child, and when the disciples ask why they were not able to do this themselves, he says, "…'Because of your little faith. Amen, I say to you, if you have faith the size of a mustard seed, you will say to the mountain, 'Move from here to there,' and it will move. Nothing will be impossible for you'" (Matthew 17: 20). I take comfort in knowing that even the great acts of life must begin by planting little seeds of trust in God.

When I give the ultimate responsibility for completing my mission to God, every conversation and action throughout the day becomes an opportunity to witness God's unconditional love to others. These days, I work as a hospital social worker on a mother-baby unit. I work with parents and families working through mental health issues, chemical dependency, domestic violence, disability issues, health issues, resource needs, immigration issues, loss, and grief. I love my job and cherish the opportunity to meet with people in times of both joy and sorrow. In my better moments, I do everything I can to offer support and connect people with ongoing community resources. There are times when the work is deeply painful and overwhelming, and there are days when I feel like a cog in a machine. Sometimes I feel like I make an impact and sometimes I feel like I run around handing out pamphlets and faxing papers that go nowhere. But regardless of how I feel, I must always remember to do my best, ask my supervisor and colleagues for advice, continually improve, give it all to God, and ask God to work through me.

Part of letting go of the false god of the search for the so-called "perfect job" was realizing how much meaning I experience through activities and relationships outside of work. For example, I volunteer with a youth group for LGBTQ and allied young people. In this community, I do my best to help build a place where everyone who walks through the door is celebrated, nurtured, included, and loved. I volunteer for various activities at my church and hope to help people experience the love of God. I write fiction and non-fiction books with hope that I can use words and stories to teach something about what love really is. And I invest time in relationships with the people I care about, my parents, my grandmothers, my sisters and brothers-in-law, my aunts, my uncles, my cousins, my friends. I share the love God gives me with the people in my life. I am not saying all of this to make myself sound like a wonderful person. Rather, I want to show you in concrete terms how I build meaning in my life through a variety of roles and relationships. Everything comes together to create the fabric of my vocation. We must all do this in our own ways. I do my best to be a good and loyal social worker, a helpful neighbor, a passionate writer, a kind youth group mentor, a loving son and brother, and a faithful disciple of Jesus Christ. I do not know what work God will call me to in the future, but I hope to always persist in my duties by remaining grounded in the Holy Spirit.

Ultimately, God is with us as we navigate our paths through life. The call will always remain to love God, love our neighbors, and love ourselves. Ask God for guidance, and trust that she will bring meaning to your life starting today. I hope you find what you are looking for.

Love,

Aaron

FOR THE DAY YOU DISCOVER A NEW PASSION

"You are the light of the world. A city set on a mountain cannot be hidden. Nor do they light a lamp and then put it under a bushel basket; it is set on a lampstand, where it gives light to all in the house. Just so, your light must shine before others, that they may see your good deeds and glorify your heavenly Father."

- Matthew 5: 14-16

Dear Brother, Dear Sister, Dear Friend,

One of the great joys of being human is discovering some cause, interest, activity, or mission that makes us feel alive in a whole new way. Such things are passions. If you have found a new one, give thanks and praise to God. He has given you an amazing gift. As is written in James 1: 17, "… all good giving and every perfect gift is from above, coming down from the Father of lights, with whom there is no alteration or shadow caused by change."

Passion can be found in many different places, and it should always lead us to love God, neighbors, and ourselves. You might delight in reading murder mysteries or baking delicious cakes. You may be enthralled with new languages or enraptured by films from a certain country. Or perhaps you suddenly feel compelled to protect tropical rainforests, fix cars, master make-up techniques, nurture

240

rescue dogs, play drums in a rock band, practice martial arts, choreograph flash mob dance routines, dive into classic Russian literature, or explore South American history. People are interesting because they care deeply about different things. We get to know others by learning what they are passionate about, and we get to know ourselves by discovering our own passions.

Some key questions might come up as you delve into something new. What is this passion for? Was it given to me exclusively for my own happiness, or is there more to it than that? Passions are gifts from God, and they come with a purpose. Any passion can be turned into an opportunity to love more deeply if we ask God to help us find a way. When we show love for others while living out the things we enjoy or care about, we simultaneously show love for our neighbors and for ourselves.

Some passions lead to clear missions. For example, someone who cares deeply about justice, freedom, and human dignity might build solidarity with survivors of human trafficking or advocate to change laws and social structures that lead to modern-day slavery. Other passions may lead less directly to a service role, but one can always be found with a little creativity. For example, people who love tiger stuffed animals can experience the fun of building a collection and then discover even greater joy by giving away adorable stuffed jungle cats to people who are sick, hurting, or lonely. Likewise, a person who loves tinkering on the piano can look for opportunities to play calming songs in hospitals, senior centers, churches, and other places where people gather. God will walk with us as we discover ways to do what we love while making the world a better place. As St. Paul writes in Galatians 5: 13-14, "For you were called for freedom, brothers. But do not use this freedom as an opportunity for the flesh; rather, serve one another through love. For the whole law is fulfilled in one statement, namely, 'You shall love your neighbor as yourself.'"

Another question that may come up is this: *Can I make a living though my passion?* Some interests clearly lead to career paths. For example, people who love math, science, and tinkering with gadgets might happily become engineers. Likewise, people fascinated by the inner workings of the human body might find their way to medical school. But other interests are typically less lucrative, such as philosophy or kickball. One could always try to be a philosophy professor or professional kickball athlete, but one might find greater satisfaction pursuing these interests outside of work. In addition, some fields are so competitive that it is difficult to find worldly professional success. This does not mean that such interests are not worth pursuing. It is nearly impossible to become a world famous actor, but one can find great meaning by bringing a character to life on a community theater stage. It is nearly impossible to become a famous painter, but motivated and inspired artists around the world create artwork that helps people in their community heal, grow, experience beauty, or learn some important truth about life. At the end of the day, some people make money while living out their passions, and some people work to support themselves so that they can do what they love for free.

The world sometimes tells us that our identities are forged exclusively through the roles we play at work and in our relationships. People say we are primarily firefighters, doctors, construction workers, teachers, sons, daughters, fathers, mothers, husbands, wives, or partners. These labels are supposed to define the totality of who we are.

Our jobs and our relationships are vital parts of our lives. Yet we must realize that all of our passions and interests come together to enrich who we are, augment the value of our professional work, and deepen our love for family, friends, neighbors, and God. For example, a business professional who loves photography could make beautiful photo collages to share with family members and colleagues. A nurse known for her patience, kindness, and tenderness might derive her spiritual strength from nights during the week when she plays guitar in a coffee shop. A police detective might be inspired to make the world a safer place by the profound love she has for her own children. God is with us as we write the stories of our lives. We must work with Him to put together the pieces of who we are and discover what we want to do with our precious time on earth. As is written in Colossians 3: 23, "Whatever you do, do from the heart, as for the Lord and not for others." Ultimately, what we do is not as important as who we are and how we live. At all times and in all things, we must choose to remain grounded in sincere love for God, tender concern for our neighbors, and joyful gratitude for our own lives.

Another question that might linger in the back of our minds is: *How can I keep my passion alive?* A new passion is a seed that needs tender love and care to grow. We must invest time, energy, and effort for a new passion to take root in our lives and thrive. Talent and interest is a great place to start with any endeavor, but we must work hard and draw our strength from God if we hope to accomplish meaningful goals. As is written in John 15: 5, "I am the vine, you are the branches. Whoever remains in me and I in him will bear much fruit, because without me you can do nothing." God will guide us where we need to be and show us how to use the passions He gives us.

For example, I love books. I have a passion for reading and I learn about life through the characters in my favorite stories. I cherish novels from a variety of genres, including classics written by women, modern young adult literature, John Newbery Medal winners, and Japanese manga from the 1990s. Over the last several years, I decided to write my own stories. It has been a journey. When I write, I feel like I am partnering with God to create something from nothing. I love writing, but it is rarely easy. I must always study to hone my craft so that my stories, ideas, and characters take on greater life and depth. To accomplish these goals, I take classes, ask friends to critique my work, read books about writing, and spend time actually putting words on paper. I do not always feel excited to write. Sometimes I feel frustrated, exhausted, or empty. But my love of writing persists even in these moments because passion is more than a feeling. It is a dedication, a commitment, a deep desire to make something part of one's life. My dream is to write books that help others learn something about God and something about love. This dream is a gift, and it will never die as long as I remain rooted in Christ.

God connects with us through our passions. When we offer our gifts, talents, interests, and missions to God, we open ourselves to the Holy Spirit. As it says in 2 Timothy 1: 7, "For God did not give us a spirit of cowardice but rather of power and love and self-control." Sadly, the world sometimes tells us that certain passions are best restricted to certain people. For example, sexist stereotypes dictate what people are supposed to pursue based on one's assigned place within a binary gender scheme. Specifically, women might be discouraged from pursing mechanics, math, sciences, and business, while men might be discouraged from pursuing fashion, art, dance, and childrearing. People who do not identify as men or women are often ignored or belittled. As gay Christians, we have a special calling to break down walls and encourage everyone to be who God created them to be. God is the one who places passion in our hearts. He does not follow human rules and prejudices. We must trust in Him and live as He calls us to live. As Jesus says in Matthew 5: 14-16, "You are the light of the world. A city set on a mountain cannot be hidden. Nor do they light a lamp and then put it under a bushel basket; it is set on a lampstand, where it gives light to all in the house. Just so, your light must shine before others, that they may see your good deeds and glorify your heavenly Father."

And so, when you discover a new passion, enjoy it. Thank God for this exciting reason to be alive. Explore how this interest fits with the other pieces of yourself, and seek ways to use what you learn for the good of others. We are all connected, and God gives each person unique gifts to be shared with neighbors for the common good. As St. Paul writes in 1 Corinthians 12: 4-7, "There are different kinds of spiritual gifts but the same Spirit; there are different forms of service but the same Lord; there are different workings but the same God who produces all of them in everyone. To each individual the manifestation of the Spirit is given for some benefit." God works through all of us to reveal His love. I am so thankful you are here. You and your passions bring depth, vibrancy, and new life to the Body of Christ.

Love,

Aaron

FOR THE DAY YOU FEEL POWERLESS TO CHANGE THE WORLD

"...then let justice surge like water, and goodness like an unfailing stream."

- Amos 5: 24

Dear Sister, Dear Brother, Dear Friend,

As followers of Christ, we are called to feed the hungry, clothe the naked, visit the sick and imprisoned, and set the captives free. We are called to care for the forests, fields, oceans, and wildlife of our precious earth. We are called to advocate for justice until human rights are universally respected and all people have what they need to survive and thrive. If we allow God to guide us, She will give us the vision and drive we need to nurture life, faith, hope, and love in every corner of the world. As Jesus says in Matthew 5: 6, "Blessed are they who hunger and thirst for righteousness, for they will be satisfied."

As caring people, our hearts break whenever we encounter suffering and injustice. Through friends, neighbors, family members, news stories, coworkers, clients, and our own lives, we encounter pain, violence, and the consequences of sin and selfishness. Every day, people endure abuse, homelessness, human trafficking, addictions, hunger, war, torture, poverty, terrorism, imperialism, crime, disease without access to health care, and policies that perpetrate racism, sexism, heterosexism, ableism, ageism, xenophobia, religious persecution, and other forms of oppression.

The misery of our broken world is oftentimes overwhelming. Because we love goodness, we wish we could do more to stop the suffering caused by evil and sin. When we do not achieve the changes we set out to make, it is easy to feel like our efforts are useless. At such times, it is helpful to turn to the words of Micah 6: 8, "You have been told, O man, what is good, and what the LORD requires of you: Only to do the right and to love goodness, and to walk humbly with your God." But sometimes loving goodness and walking humbly with God does not feel like enough. We want to do more. We ask, *How can we make a real impact when the world's needs are so numerous and deep? How can we solve problems when the root causes are buried in complicated webs of history, politics, oppression, and sin?* Doubt seeps in, and the greatest temptation becomes to do nothing.

This is how the forces of evil want us to feel. When we believe we are powerless, we reject the opportunities God gives us to build solidarity with others and make a positive impact. Dwelling on our own inadequacies numbs us to pain until we stop caring. If we give in to this, it becomes easy to abandon the humble works of love that God made us to do.

We must never give up hope because even amidst weakness and defeat we have God. As it says in 2 Corinthians 12: 10, "Therefore, I am content with weaknesses, insults, hardships, persecutions, and constraints, for the sake of Christ; for when I am weak, then I am strong." True power comes when we acknowledge our weakness and surrender everything to God. As human beings, we are not able to solve the world's problems on our own. Rather, we must give our lives, hopes, dreams, desires, and visions to God and ask Her to guide us in doing our part to reform the world. God alone has the wisdom, mercy, gentleness, power, and strength to heal this planet and its people. God will share all these things and more with us if we go to Her and dwell in the power of Her love.

When we give ourselves over to God, we become the Body of Christ alive in the world today. She is able to work through our reason, resources, efforts, virtues, passions, coalitions, institutions, communities, and everything we are to restore goodness, beauty, and truth. The work of redemption that began with the life, death, and resurrection of Christ continues in us today. Christians throughout the ages must carry on until the promised day when, in the words of Revelation 21: 4, "He will wipe every tear from their eyes, and there shall be no more death or mourning, wailing or pain, for the old order has passed away."

The important thing is to never give up even if we feel overwhelmed by the immensity of human suffering, the imbedded nature of unjust social structures, or our own feelings failure. Revered spiritual leader, humanitarian, and activist Mother Teresa once said, "If you can't feed a hundred people, then feed just one" (Costello, 2008, p. 13). As we struggle and strive for justice, we must find satisfaction in small victories. If we do not look for little moments of healing or growth, we may never see any results at all. Sometimes all we can do is plant seeds of reconciliation, peace, or hope, and then trust that God and others will take over the work from there. It is the love we bring to our work that matters, and it is the power of love that will unite our efforts in bringing forth the Kingdom of God.

As human beings, we are not saviors. God is the one true Savior. When people act as if they are responsible for solving everyone's problems, this often opens the door to abuse of power, misunderstandings, exploitation, and violence. If we hope to establish peace and justice, we must follow God's lead and form genuine partnerships with others, including those we hope to serve. Our God is everyone's God. We all share equal dignity through being made in God's image. We must allow God to transform our lives, change the aspects of our lifestyles that cause harm, and bring us together to work in solidarity for a better world. With God's help, we can do a lot of good by simply minimizing the resources we use, choosing consumer goods that are not produced through slavery or sweatshop labor, and being kind and generous to the people we encounter in day to day life. If we start there, God will show us more and more ways to serve and work toward positive social change. Ultimately, we are called to love God, love our neighbors, and love ourselves. If everyone truly loved their neighbors starting today, the world would radically change in a moment. We would begin to see more clearly the vision of Amos 5: 24, "…then let justice surge like water, and goodness like an unfailing stream."

Of course, we can tell ourselves all day that we need to entrust everything to God, but there will still be moments when the pain of others overwhelms us. In my work as a social worker, there are days when I feel like everything I do is useless. As a child and family therapist, I worked with young clients who faced depression. Some of them were suicidal and could not even get out of bed. I had other clients who had survived abuse and were acting out in school through tantrums, fighting, and defiance of teachers. I worked with my clients week after week, empathized with their feelings, offered new ways of looking at things, affirmed their strengths, discussed parenting strategies with caregivers, and asked questions to help clients think about what they wanted and needed in life. I did everything I was taught to do, but there were many times when it seemed like nothing made an impact. My clients were still too depressed to get out of bed, thinking about killing themselves, and fighting with teachers and families. I could not take their pain away, and I could not change the circumstances that hurt them. They faced poverty, racism, sexism, heterosexism, past trauma, and demons of self-loathing and anger. What was I supposed to do? Through conversations with supervisors, professors, mentors, colleagues, family, and friends, God helped me see that all I could do was show up faithfully to meetings, support my clients the best I could, and pray for them. They did not need me to save them. They needed God, and they needed to find Her in their own way and in their own time. I hope I was a small piece of their journey through healing and growth, but for their good, I still wish I could have done more. And I think that is okay. As compassionate human beings who care about people and the world, there will be times when we suffer. It is better to hurt with others than to ignore their pain. God suffers with us when we suffer, and so we are never alone.

As gay Christians, we have keen insight into some particularly painful issues that impact our world. We see preachers and youth ministers teach hateful ideas about gay people. We see young people being used for sex by adults twice their age or older. We see youth bullied or rejected by peers. We see people trapped in abusive relationships who believe they do not deserve to be treated with kindness or respect. We see homeless people, young and old, who have been run out of their homes because of their sexual orientations or gender identities. Drug and alcohol use is an epidemic in some gay scenes as people seek escape from shame, trauma, or rejection, or rather seek community and happiness without realizing that substances ultimately lead to pain. Promiscuous sex becomes a quick and insufficient substitute for deep yearnings of connection, love, and belonging, which often results in broken hearts and painful infections. So many of us and our gay, lesbian, bisexual, transgender, queer, and questioning brothers, sisters, and friends struggle with severe economic, social, medical, and mental health needs. We often lack access to basic resources, supportive environments, medical care, and healthy, loving communities that nurture us in being ourselves and growing into the people God made us to be.

All this pain and injustice needs to stop. We need leaders to rise up, preach the gospel of love, and live it out in everyday life. We must envision a future where all people are protected, cared for, and cherished. When you feel overwhelmed by the trauma of your own life or the forces of evil, step back from the world as it is and dream of the world as it could be. Picture young people growing up in homes and churches that celebrate who they are. Think about soul mates finding each other and being good to each other. Envision good people opening their homes to youth who need families. Draw strength from your dreams and open your eyes to moments where seeds of redemption are being planted in your life. Do not despair, for in all things, Jesus Christ is our reason for hope. He has already defeated sin, death, and evil through his crucifixion and resurrection. We have the opportunity to work beside him today as we build up his kingdom, brick by brick, one mended heart at a time. We cannot always see it, but we must believe it and place trust not in ourselves, but in God. Romans 8: 24-25 says, "For in hope we were saved. Now hope that sees for itself is not hope. For who hopes for what one sees? But if we hope for what we do not see, we wait with endurance."

Please, do not give in to despair. Proclaim the good news of Jesus Christ by word and deed. God became human so that we might all be saved. Through our suffering we die with him, but with him we also rise. Remember the words of Romans 12: 21: "Do not be conquered by evil but conquer evil with good." Keep going. Keep fighting. Keep living. Keep loving. There will come a day when all will be made new, and we will see God and Her goodness face to face.

Love,

Aaron

FOR THE DAY YOU ARE FILLED WITH THE HOLY SPIRIT OF THE LIVING GOD

"Then the LORD said, 'Go outside and stand on the mountain before the LORD; the LORD will be passing by.' A strong and heavy wind was rending the mountains and crushing rocks before the LORD— but the LORD was not in the wind. After the wind there was an earthquake— but the LORD was not in the earthquake. After the earthquake there was fire— but the LORD was not in the fire. After the fire there was a tiny whispering sound. When he heard this, Elijah hid his face in his cloak and went and stood at the entrance of the cave…"

\- 1 Kings 19: 11-13A

Dear Brother, Dear Sister, Dear Friend,

As Christians, we are graced with the knowledge that God's Holy Spirit is present in the world and in each of us. She is sometimes portrayed symbolically through fire, wind, or in the form of a dove. These images seek to capture the passion, freedom, and rushing joy of the Holy Spirit of God, who is the source of all love and all life.

I am happy that today you are filled with God's Holy Spirit. You are in good company. Some encounter the Spirit in Scripture study or worship services at church. Others find the Holy Spirit through art, literature, music, or dance. Many find the Spirit of God through contemplating the beauty of nature or the goodness of family, friends, and neighbors. Many others grow closer to the Spirit through daily work, loving acts of kindness, or efforts to build justice. The truth is that a deep connection with God can be found through all things because God, the source of creativity and meaning, is present in all good human endeavors and all of Creation. If we let her, the Holy Spirit will join us wherever we are, guide us, deepen the value of our work, and enrich the joy of our lives.

If your current experience of intimacy with the Spirit is new or unfamiliar, you may be wondering, *How can I trust that this is real? What is really happening here?* As long as your experience is leading you to deeper love of God, neighbors, and yourself, then enjoy the ride and try to let go of fear and doubt. Jesus promised that God would send the Holy Spirit to help us live rightly. In John 14: 16-17, Jesus says, "And I will ask the Father, and he will give you another Advocate to be with you always, the Spirit of truth, which the world cannot accept, because it neither sees nor knows it. But you know it, because it remains with you, and will be in you." Jesus promises that God will send upon us the Holy Spirit, unseen by worldly eyes but known intimately as a friend and ally by those who open their hearts to receive her.

As a young man, I experienced the sacrament of Confirmation. As I was anointed with oil and given a new spiritual name, I committed myself to Christ and opened my heart to the Holy Spirit in a new way. At that time, I was on the brink of adulthood and about to embark on a new chapter of life. I yearned to serve my neighbors and I wanted to dedicate myself to God. The sacrament of Confirmation and similar rituals in churches all over the world seek to live out the words of Romans 12: 1-2: "I urge you therefore, brothers, by the mercies of God, to offer your bodies as a living sacrifice, holy and pleasing to God, your spiritual worship. Do not conform yourself to this age but be transformed by the renewal of your mind, that you may discern what is the will of God, what is good and pleasing and perfect."

I feel the Holy Spirit moving in my heart and soul every day. Sometimes I experience a rush of joy that begins in my chest then zings into my head and throughout my entire body. Sometimes I discover quiet moments of peace as new spiritual insights or understandings dawn upon me. Sometimes the Spirit brings me a sense of freedom as I either embrace some mission or take a step into the unknown.

If we seek direction and peace from the Holy Spirit, she will never let us down. As a gay man, I believed for a long time that I had to be celibate for my entire life if I wanted to be a faithful Christian. Rather than bringing me peace, this notion led to despair and misery. It seemed like I had nothing substantial to hope for and my only consolation was found in thoughts of dying and going to heaven. The wise counsel of many good people, Scripture study, and countless days and nights of prayer culminated in a retreat where I encountered this prayer by Catholic monk and spiritual writer, Thomas Merton (2005):

> My Lord God, I have no idea where I am going. I do not see the road ahead of me. I cannot know for certain where it will end. Nor do I really know myself, and the fact that I think that I am following your will does not mean that I am actually doing so. But I believe that the desire to please you does in fact please you. And I hope I have that desire in all that I am doing. I hope that I will never do anything apart from that desire. And I know that if I do this you will lead me by the right road though I may know nothing about it. Therefore will I trust you always though I may seem to be lost and in the shadow of death. I will not fear, for you are ever with me, and you will never leave me to face my perils alone. (pp. 57-58)

I meditated on the words of this prayer as I walked through a path in the forest. As I inhaled the cool scent of pine trees in the twilight, I felt the presence of the Holy Spirit grow stronger and stronger in my heart. A quiet voice opened my eyes to the reality that God is love and that wherever there is love, there is God. The words of

Merton's prayer echoed in my heart along with the encouragement of mentors and the words of Romans 13: 8: "Owe nothing to anyone, except to love one another; for the one who loves another has fulfilled the law." For the first time in my life, I believed that it might be possible for God to call me to a loving relationship with a good man. Hope is found when we dwell in possibilities for good. The Holy Spirit lives, moves, and breathes through such possibilities.

On that forest trail, I knew that God might still call me to the single life, and I remained committed to following God wherever He led me. But even knowing that, the future had lost its bleak emptiness. For the first time since realizing I was gay, I had hope that I could find joy and peace this side of heaven. The future had yet to be decided, and there was a good God beside me helping me to find my way. All I had to do was love the best I could. Whatever came to pass, joy and peace were already alive inside of me. I learned that life did not become good when circumstances changed. Life is good now because God loves me and I love Him. The Holy Spirit moved my heart, and I became a new man. My eyes were opened to so many opportunities for love starting that day. I had my family, my friends, my work, my writing, and my God. I had so many blessings and so many ways to serve. I never wanted to let despair steal my spirit ever again.

That walk through the woods was a moment in my life when the Holy Spirit made her presence boldly known. Maybe you have encountered the Spirit in similar moments, but oftentimes she is more gentle and subtle. We read about Elijah's encounter with God in 1 Kings 19: 11-13A: "Then the LORD said, 'Go outside and stand on the mountain before the LORD; the LORD will be passing by.' A strong and heavy wind was rending the mountains and crushing rocks before the LORD— but the LORD was not in the wind. After the wind there was an earthquake— but the LORD was not in the earthquake. After the earthquake there was fire— but the LORD was not in the fire. After the fire there was a tiny whispering sound. When he heard this, Elijah hid his face in his cloak and went and stood at the entrance of the cave…" Elijah went outside to meet with the Holy Spirit of God, who was present not in mighty acts of power but in the "tiny whispering sound." We find great peace when we listen to the quiet voice of the Spirit and let her speak love, truth, and mercy to our hearts. If you feel anxious about the tasks that lay before you, afraid of the enemies that threaten you, overwhelmed by the duties placed upon you, or lost in a sea of confusion or suffering, then open your heart and listen to the whispering voice of the Holy Spirit. Let her become your peace and calm amidst the storms of life, and allow her to show you the way home.

When you experience a moment of connection with the Holy Spirit, hold onto it. Let it nurture within you an ongoing, loving relationship with God. We are made to be Temples of the Holy Spirit so that God may live and love in the world through us. When we live grounded in this truth, other people notice. As it says in Galatians 5: 22-23, "In contrast, the fruit of the Spirit is love, joy peace, patience, kindness, generosity, faithfulness, gentleness, self-control. Against such there is no law." When these are the fundamental markings of our character, people will be drawn to our way of life and we will have opportunities to share the good news of redemption and love. The world changes for the better when people let the Spirit of God move and breathe in their hearts.

As you live, let your choices flow from your relationship with the Holy Spirit. Do not make decisions based on cringing fear, ignorant prejudices, or selfish thoughts of worldly gain. Center yourself in God's Spirit through prayer, Scripture study, community worship, art, music, poetry, good works, and acts of justice. Let her be your anchor and your guiding light. Trust in the revelations she has made to the world through the Bible and through the saints, and live in such a way that your life is a testimony to her love and peace.

Perhaps you have had moments of connection with the Holy Spirit in the past but now you feel distant and spiritually dry. First of all, this is completely normal.

Feelings come and go. That is part of the human experience. The important thing to remember is to choose to love God, love others, and love yourself faithfully through the emotional ups, downs, and deserts of life. When we choose love in the difficult or empty times, this is a sacred opportunity to prove to ourselves and to God that we love because it is right, not only because it makes us feel good. Even when we do not feel the Holy Spirit, she is always with us. We can trust her no matter what because we know that she loves us. If we remain open and faithful, feelings of her presence and grace will always return in time.

Please, pray with me today that the Holy Spirit of the living God comes upon us all. Consecrate your hands, your feet, your heart, your life, your everything to God. Let the Holy Spirit of love fill you and transform you into a member of the Body of Christ. Allow her to heal your wounds, refresh your soul, and dwell deep within you so that God will live in all you do, chase away every fear, and guide you on the path of righteousness and mercy.

Love,

Aaron

ONE FINAL LETTER OF GRATITUDE

"Give thanks to the LORD, for he is good, for his kindness endures forever…"

-1 Chronicles 16: 34

Dear Brother, Dear Sister, Dear Friend,

As I write the final pages of this book, I find myself overwhelmed by the many blessings that fill my life with joy and meaning. I am thankful to my family for loving me no matter what. I thank my parents for showing me that true purpose is rooted in self-sacrificing love, and I thank my sisters for being my strongest allies. This book would not exist without the love, support, and practical help of my family. I am grateful for friends who make me laugh and always have my back. I am thankful for the teachers who opened my eyes to the power of literature, the demands of justice, and the importance of truth. I am thankful for young people everywhere whose courage inspires me to keep going. And most of all, I thank God for giving us life, carrying us through the storms, and lighting the path to a better world.

Thank you for reading this book. I hope you found some comfort and wisdom in its pages. God loves you, and so do I. May the good Lord bless you with peace and joy on your journey.

Love,

Aaron

Works Cited

Bass, E. (2002). *Mules of love*. Rochester, NY: BOA Editions, Ltd.

Costello, G. (2008). *Spiritual Gems from mother teresa*. New London, CT: Twenty-Third Publications. Used with permission granted by Twenty-Third Publications, New London, Connecticut.

Ellen Bass, "The Thing Is" from *Mules of Love*. Copyright © 2002 by Ellen Bass. Reprinted with the permission of The Permissions Company, Inc., on behalf of BOA Editions Ltd., www.boaeditions.org

Fuller, S. (1905). *How Helen Keller was taught speech*. Washington, DC: Press of Gibson Brothers.

Graham, W. C. (2014). *100 days closer to Christ*. Collegeville, MN: Liturgical Press. © 2014 by Order of Saint Benedict, Collegeville, Minnesota. Used with permission.

Keller, H. (2003). *The world I live in*. R. Shattuck (Ed.). New York, NY: New York Review Books.

Kierkegaard, S. (1962). *Works of love: Some Christian reflections in the form of discourses*. Translated by Howard and Edna Hong. New York, NY: Harper Torchbooks.

Merton, T. (2005). *I have seen what I was looking for: Selected spiritual writings*. M. B. Pennington (Ed.). Hyde Park, NY: New City Press.

Teresa, M. (1996). *In my own words*. J. L. Gonzalez-

Balado (Ed.). Liguori, MO: Liguori Publications.
Excerpt from *Mother Teresa: In My Own Words* ©
1996 Liguori Publications liguori.org Used with
Permission. All rights reserved.

Wolf, N. (2002). *The beauty myth: How images of beauty are used against women.* New York, NY: HarperCollins Publishers.

About the Author

Aaron Walsh is thankful to be a young gay Christian. He spends his days working as a social worker for a family childbirth center and his nights writing. One of the greatest joys of his life is volunteering with an LGBTQ-and-allied youth group in his hometown.

It took Aaron several years to reconcile his Christian religious beliefs with his sexual orientation. Through prayer, study, and long conversations with God, he has been graced with understanding and insights that he hopes to share with others. He feels a strong sense of mission to preach the gospel of love, healing, and redemption to everyone he meets. Aaron hopes to help people everywhere experience the essential truth that God is love. You can email Aaron at letterstoayounggaychristian@gmail.com.

89441638R00166

Made in the USA
San Bernardino, CA
25 September 2018